DOWN
TO
EARTH
THE LAWS OF THE HARVEST

by
John W. Lawrence

Multnomah Press
Portland, Ore. 97266

INTERNATIONAL STANDARD BOOK NUMBER:
0-930014-04-9

LIBRARY OF CONGRESS NUMBER:
77-7731

First Printing: 1975
Second Printing: 1977
Printed in USA

Dedicated to
Dr. John G. Mitchell
who has faithfully labored
and I have entered into his labors

FOREWORD

God has seen fit to reveal Himself to us through nature (Romans 1:20; Psalm 19:1). It was God's revelation of Himself through this means that brought Job an understanding, both of himself and of God (Job 38–42). Christ frequently made reference to nature to teach some truth to His disciples (John 12:24), and many of His parables are drawn from the natural realm (Matthew 13:3-9).

John Lawrence, following this principle has outlined seven laws which operate in the natural realm in the area of sowing and harvesting. Then with perception he has shown that these same laws operate in the spiritual realm as well.

Believers recognize that they are responsible to produce the "peaceable fruit of righteousness" (Hebrews 12:11). Christ commanded them to be bearing fruit (John 15:16). Few recognize the laws which operate to produce that which is commanded. Lawrence makes these laws very practical and plain. His many illustrations bring the truth home to the mind and heart.

One who recognizes these laws and puts them into operation in his life by the power of the Spirit will surely note an increase in the harvest in his life. May the Lord use these pages to that end.

–J. Dwight Pentecost
Chairman of Department of Bible Exposition
Dallas Theological Seminary

TABLE OF CONTENTS

INTRODUCTION

The agonizing cry of Hosea, the Old Testament prophet, "My people are destroyed for lack of knowledge"
(Hosea 4:6), needs to resound again in our day across the
land. As a people, many of us do not know the Bible,
God's Word, and even more have never known the God of
the Word; but His Word still stands. Truth marches on; and
truth always triumphs, often at the expense of the people
who are careless of it and indifferent to it. God give us ears
to hear both in the church and in the world! As never
before, we need to heed the voice of God as He speaks in
and through His Word. We have flaunted God, and our
arrogance is coming back upon us. To be ignorant is bad
enough, but to be arrogant as well, is double sin. The Word
of God can change our ignorance; the Spirit of God, our
arrogance.

The Word never changes, but insight into what the
Word teaches continually increases under the teaching and
illuminating ministry of the Spirit of God. Our need today
is not for more Bible translations in the English language,
as good as they may be. We need rather to read and heed
what the Bible does say to us in our generation. As
someone phrased it: "The Bible does not need to be
rewritten, but reread." One of the cardinal truths for the

Christian is that within the Bible is all that is necessary for faith and for practice. The believer who knows the Scripture and patterns his life by it has found this to be true.

Our prayer, then, should be that of the Psalmist: "Open thou mine eyes, that I may behold wondrous things out of thy law" (Psalms 119:18). In reference to the subject of sowing and reaping, Scripture teaches far more than the facts that you reap what you sow and you reap in a different season. There are other laws, which any farmer knows, that equally apply, and these are just as functional in the spiritual realm as they are in the natural. In fact, if the farmer knew no more about the principles of farming than the average Christian does about producing a spiritual harvest, he would never make it through the winter. God is a God of order, and everything He does is orderly according to fixed laws of operation. If this were not true, none of our astronauts would have walked on the moon; for all that was involved in this procedure depended upon the minute accuracy of movement, propellants and equipment. Have we forgotten that God's universe is one, and that the laws in the spiritual realm are equally as fixed and functional as in the physical? Man can no more make these laws than Newton could make the law of gravity; he can only discover these laws by which He operates on earth. Yet the Word of God teems with these laws. The scientific advancement of this century is due to the fact that man has learned to utilize the established laws that exist in the universe. In just the same way, man needs both to know the spiritual laws of God and to govern his life according to them if he would prosper and advance spiritually.

Spiritual Laws in Scripture

An example of God's working according to set principles may be seen in the four basic laws that have to do with sin and evil. First, there is the law of the perpetual evil of the sin nature. One of the first things the young Christian needs to learn is that there is no good in the old nature. Even the tendency within older believers is to forget this. Jeremiah 17:9 says: "The heart is deceitful above all things, and desperately wicked." The very same word translated "desperately" here is translated in Jeremiah 30:12 and 15 as "incurably." The heart of man is, literally, "incurably wicked."

Moreover, it is not God's program to change the evil heart and nature of man. Rather, His program is the creation within man of an entirely new being—a new birth, a new creation. It may be said, then, that the Lord is not in the business of reformation, but of regeneration. It is not our turning over a new leaf, but His giving us a new life. In fact, we cannot be saved until we have given up all hope of saving ourselves or even of working along with God in our salvation. God's work of salvation is all His. "Salvation is of the Lord" (Jonah 2:9). It is 100 percent of the Lord, not 99 and 44/100's percent His and 56/100's percent ours. And the reason it is all of Him is "that no flesh should glory in His presence" (1 Corinthians 1:29). So we find that we are saved "by grace . . . through faith; and that not of yourselves: it is the gift of God: not of works, lest any man should boast" (Ephesians 2:8-9). God's message is that "not by works of righteousness which we have done, but according to his mercy he saved us" (Titus 3:5). His verdict upon all our righteousness is that they are "filthy rags" (Isaiah 64:6). This is God's view of our righteousness to say nothing of what He thinks about our sins and iniquities. The best the flesh can do cannot stand in the presence of a holy and righteous God. All that the old nature of man can do is like in kind to itself. It is all evil and vile before God. It is perpetually evil.

Second, there is the law of continual conflict. This principle is seen in Galatians 5 where Paul brings out that there will always be continual conflict between what the flesh nature wants and what the Holy Spirit of God wants. He says in verse 17, "For the flesh lusteth against the Spirit, and the Spirit against the flesh, and these are contrary the one to the other: so that ye cannot do the things that ye would." Whatever the flesh desires is just contrary to what the Holy Spirit desires; and what the Holy Spirit wants, the flesh never wants.

Since these are literally opposites the one to the other, at no time do both of them get together and want the same thing. There is no summit conference in which they meet and talk this thing over. There is no détente. Now, the net result is that the believer has within him continual conflict just as long as he is living in the body. This conflict never existed before he was saved, because then he only had one nature—a sin nature. But being saved and having the indwelling Holy Spirit and a new nature, the child of God finds he cannot do anything without opposition. If we choose the Spirit's way, the flesh opposes. If we choose the way of the flesh, the Spirit opposes.

But God's program is for each believer to walk in the Spirit and so not to fulfill the lust of the flesh (Galatians 5:16). The flesh remains, along with the world and the devil, as one of the three enemies the child of God faces until he sees the Lord and becomes like Him (1 John 3:2). Not only does it remain, but it continually seeks to oppose what the Holy Spirit of God wants to do in the believer's life.

Another law clearly seen in Scripture is the law of leaven. This is the fact that any time sin of any variety is allowed to exist and is not dealt with by the believer, that sin continues to work as leaven until the whole is corrupted. "A little leaven leaveneth the whole lump" (Galatians 5:9). If we do not deal with sin, it will deal with us. This law only works one way, however. Good apples never change the bad apples, but just the reverse. As Paul expressed it: "Evil companions tear down good morals" (1 Corinthians 15:33, literal translation).

A fourth law in the area of sin is the law of temporal death, which simply is the fact that whenever the child of God is operating through the sin nature he is in a state of temporal death before God. This has nothing to do with having lost his salvation, but rather of having broken his fellowship. A sinning child is still a child of his father, but his sinning against him will break fellowship with him. So Paul says, "To be carnally minded is death; but to be spiritually minded is life and peace" (Romans 8:6). He says, moreover, "She that liveth in pleasure is dead while she liveth" (1 Timothy 5:6). Many of God's children are living in a state of temporal death before God. They are not living in communion with the Lord, and so are not producing the fruit that can only be produced through an abiding life (cf. John 15; 1 John 1).

Laws for the Galatians

These are but an example of the laws Scripture gives of God's operation in the spiritual realm. There are laws governing man and his makeup, concerning spiritual development and maturity to mention just a few. But there are no laws more important or significant to us than the principles that govern the harvest we reap. In the book of Galatians, Paul has been dealing with one principle—the Galatians are not under the law of Moses or any legal system, either to be saved or to live pleasing to God. Having driven this point home for five chapters, Paul then says to these Galatian believers: "Be not deceived; God is not mocked: for whatsoever a man soweth, that shall he also reap. For he that soweth to his flesh shall of the flesh reap corruption; but he that soweth to the Spirit shall of the Spirit reap life everlasting. And let us not be weary in well doing: for in due season we shall reap, if we faint not. As we have therefore opportunity, let us do good unto all men, especially unto them who are of the household of faith" (Galatians 6:7-10).

While those believers were not under the law that God gave from Sinai or any other legal code that man might adopt for righteousness; yet still they were under the spiritual laws of God's operation, and they dare not deceive themselves to the contrary.

We today in this age of "grace" need this truth brought forcibly home to us. Somewhere we have developed the idea that we can do anything wrong and then use 1 John 1:9, and we will get by with it. In doing this, we are deceiving ourselves and making a mockery of God and His Word. Paul says these laws operate today; they are inviolable; they change for no one; they are absolute and unfailing. These laws of sowing and reaping are equally valid for all, whether we are married or single, male or female, young or old, rich or poor, or any other distinction we might make. In fact, these laws operate whether we know about them or are totally ignorant of them. While earth remains, no man will mock God by changing for even one time these laws of the harvest. They are seven in number.

The Seven Laws of the Harvest

LAW #1.   **WE REAP ONLY WHAT HAS BEEN SOWN.** All life comes from antecedent life; for as Louis Pasteur has adequately demonstrated, there is no such thing as spontaneous generation. What we reap, then, was planted either naturally or purposely, either by God or man, for either positive or negative results. We are benefactors of much for which we have extended no labor, but we enter into the labor of others. We are recipients also of the sowing of tares in the field; for what others do does affect us, and there is no way for us to elude it.

LAW #2.   **WE REAP THE SAME IN KIND AS WE SOW.** Whatever we sow, we reap; so that, if we sow the good, we will reap the good. If we sow the evil, we will reap the evil.

LAW #3.   **WE REAP IN A DIFFERENT SEASON THAN WHEN WE SOW.** We sow in one season; we reap in another. No harvest comes the moment the seed is planted, but it must await God's appointed time.

LAW #4. **WE REAP MORE THAN WE SOW.**
No fact is more significant and sobering. When we sow the wind, we reap the whirlwind. When we sow good, we bountifully receive from the hand of God who is debtor to no man; for the harvest is always greater than the seed planted. If this were not the case, no farmer would plant anything.

LAW #5. **WE REAP IN PROPORTION AS WE SOW.**
If we sow sparingly, we reap sparingly; but if we sow bountifully, we reap accordingly. The more ground we sow, the greater harvest we will have.

LAW #6. **WE REAP THE FULL HARVEST OF THE GOOD ONLY IF WE PERSEVERE; THE EVIL COMES TO HARVEST ON ITS OWN.**
Weeds grow by themselves, but this is not true with the vegetables in the garden. These require much care.

LAW #7. **WE CANNOT DO ANYTHING ABOUT LAST YEAR'S HARVEST, BUT WE CAN ABOUT THIS YEAR'S.**
Last year is a fact of history that cannot be relived and about which we can do nothing. Our concern needs to be for what we are producing right now.

1

CONSIDERING

LAW #1   WE REAP ONLY WHAT HAS BEEN SOWN.

Stop and think: Much that we reap, we never planted. Somebody else did, and we reap the consequences. Sometimes we reap things that are good, but not always. If others have sown tares in our field, at the time of reaping there is no way around reaping the consequences. This is the first basic law of the harvest.

LAW #1.   WE REAP ONLY WHAT HAS BEEN SOWN.

The implications of this fact are staggering. On the positive side of the ledger we receive many blessings given to us by God for which we have performed no labor whatever. In fact, the Lord wants us to trust Him that He will provide all of our needs even as He provides for the birds of the air (Matthew 6:25-34). The Lord extends His blessings to all men as "he maketh his sun to rise on the evil and on the good, and sendeth rain on the just and on the unjust" (Matthew 5:45). God is gracious toward all men whether they realize it or not, or whether they ever give thanks to Him for His provisions.

He is "the living God, which made heaven, and earth, and the sea, and all things that are therein: who . . . left not himself without witness, in that he did good, and gave us rain from heaven and earth . . . he giveth to all life, and breath, and all things . . . in him we live, and move, and have our being . . ." (Acts 17:24-28). As the prophet Isaiah said, ". . . the rain cometh down, and the snow from heaven, and returneth not thither, but watereth the earth, and maketh it bring forth and bud, that it may give seed to the sower, and bread to the eater" (Isaiah 55:10). It may be that one plants, another waters, but God causes the seed to grow (cf. 1 Corinthians 3:6).

But what is God's indictment against mankind? It is namely that "because that, when they knew God, they glorified him not as God, neither were thankful . . ." (Romans 1:21). They are guilty of ingratitude. What man did, rather than give thanks to God, was change "the truth of God into a lie," and worship and serve the creature "more than the Creator" (Romans 1:25).

Yet God loved man. The greatest giver of all is God Himself. He loves to give. He is a God that is abundant in mercy. "Every good act of giving and every complete and perfect gift is from above, descending from the Father of lights, with whom is no variation or shadow cast by turning" (James 1:17, literal translation). "A man can receive nothing, except it be given him from heaven" (John 3:27).

The greatest of all gifts is the gift of the Father's own Son. "Last of all he sent unto them his Son" (Matthew 21:37). "For God so loved the world that he gave," not just anything, but his very best; "He gave his only begotten Son." Why did He give Him? He gave Him to die a substitutionary death on the cross "that whosoever believeth in him should not perish, but have everlasting life" (John 3:16). Nothing can be greater than this because nothing is greater than this.

So the Father gives salvation to all who do nothing more than believe on His Son. "For God sent not his Son into the world to condemn the world; but that the world through him might be saved" (John 3:17). "If we receive the witness of men, the witness of God is greater: for this is the witness of God which he hath testified of his Son. He that believeth on the Son of God hath the witness in himself: he that believeth not God hath made him a liar; because he believeth not the record that God gave of his Son. And this is the record, that God hath given to us eternal life, and this life is in his Son. He that hath the Son hath life; and he that hath not the Son of God hath not life" (1 John 5:9-12).

We either believe the witness God has given concerning His Son that salvation is only in and through Him or we are still trying to be saved by and through our own deeds of righteousness. Yet the message from God is "for by grace are ye saved through faith; and that not of yourselves: it is the gift of God: not of works, lest any man should boast" (Ephesians 2:8-9). And we would boast—all of us would—if we, in any way, could contribute to our eternal salvation. But God has no program of ever saving us as long as we are going to try to *do* anything.

After a series of meetings had finished, Billy Sunday was helping the workmen take down the tent when a young man who had been in the meeting the night before, now greatly under conviction, came up to Mr. Sunday earnestly inquiring: "What must I do to be saved?"

Billy's reply was startling, "You are too late," he said and kept on working.

"Oh, do not say that," exclaimed the young man, "for I earnestly desire salvation; I would do anything or go anywhere to obtain it."

"I cannot help it," came the reply. "You are too late; for your salvation was completed many years ago by Jesus Christ, and it is a finished work. All you have to do is simply accept it. You have done nothing and can do nothing to merit salvation. It is free to all who will receive it." The man believed and was saved.

God is asking you to receive something for which you extended no labor, and for which you have no merit or standing. You must receive it God's way or you will not receive it at all.

> I am not skilled to understand
>> What God hath willed, what God hath planned;
> I only know at His right hand
>> Is One who is my Savior!
>
> I take Him at His word indeed:
>> 'Christ died for sinners,' this I read;
> For in my heart I find a need
>> Of Him to be my Savior!
>
> That He should leave His place on high
>> And come for sinful man to die,
> You count it strange? so once did I,
>> Before I knew my Savior!
>> —Dora Greenwell

But not only are we blessed because of what God has done in our behalf, we are also blessed by what others have done. Others have labored and we have entered into the blessings of their labors. Any honest study of Western civilization must admit that the blessings we have enjoyed in the Western world, of freedom, of law, of ministering to the suffering, the poor and the like, are all the by-products of Christianity. Others have labored, and we have entered into the blessings of their labors in the establishment of churches, schools, orphanages, hospitals and all the many other blessings we enjoy so bountifully.

A good number of years ago there appeared in the "Christian Advocate" the following:

"America rests upon four corner stones: the English Bible, the English language, the common law, and the tradition of liberty. But liberty, language, and law might have been drawn from the Bible alone. Had we brought nothing with us across the sea besides this supreme Book, we might still have been great. Without this Book, America could not have become what she is and when she loses its guidance and wisdom, she will be America no more.

"Did we bring the Bible to these shores? Did it not rather bring us? The breath of ancient Prophets was in the sails that drove the tiny *Mayflower.* The hope and faith of ancient poets, kings, and lawgivers were in the hearts of those who first sang the Lord's song in this strange land. Our first dim outlines of a commonwealth in the Western world were drawn 'as near as might be to that which was the glory of Israel.'

"From those beginnings until now the Bible has been a teacher to our best men, a rebuke to our worst, and a noble companion to us all."

It has been said that South America was settled by the Spanish, who came to that land in search of gold, but North America was settled by the Pilgrim Fathers, who came in search of God. That is what made the difference.

Even though much has eroded away of the blessings of our heritage, yet much still remains. It is true in each of our churches that others have labored before us and sown good seed, and now we come along and enjoy the benefits of their labors. So likewise many faithful pastors, Christian workers, missionaries and Sunday school teachers have faithfully sown the seed around the world, and along comes someone else and reaps the benefits; yet each man will have his own reward according to his own labor in the Lord.

This principle is brought out and developed by the Lord Jesus Christ Himself in John 4 when He says to His disciples: "Say not ye, There are yet four months, and then cometh harvest? behold, I say unto you, Lift up your eyes, and look on the fields; for they are white already to harvest. And he that reapeth receiveth wages, and gathereth fruit unto life eternal: that both he that soweth and he that reapeth may rejoice together. And herein is that saying true, One soweth, and another reapeth. I sent you to reap that whereon ye bestowed no labour: other men laboured, and ye are entered into their labours" (John 4:35-38).

The principle is: Let us do what we can while we can and leave the results with God. Some may be involved in sowing seed, others in reaping the harvest only because others have sown. The man who has the glorious privilege of reaping may not have labored much at all; and, therefore, his reward will be very little in comparison to the one who has faithfully sown and watered the seed. God's principle is stated clearly in Ephesians 6:8, "Knowing that whatsoever good thing any man doeth, the same shall he receive of the Lord, whether he be bond or free." Therefore we are to do all the good we can to everyone because we do not know how long we have to labor. "In the morning sow thy seed, and in the evening withhold not thine hand: for thou knowest not whether shall prosper, either this or that, or whether they both shall be alike good" (Ecclesiastes 11:6).

The Negative Aspects of This Law

This law operates not only positively, but also negatively. Let me explain. We not only enter into blessings God has bestowed upon us for which we have not labored at all, and we not only enter into the blessings and benefits of the labors of others in this life, but we reap the wrong because others came along before us and sowed the wrong.

Individually, our parents may have sown within us a critical spirit. Perhaps they were always finding fault with everything, and we learned to imitate them and criticize things and people. They may have had a poor self-image and have given to us the same. They may have been fearful and afraid, and so this is the way we have become in life.

But there are other ways we can reap the wrong. When someone is murdered in our area, we may say, "This is no concern to me. Let me just go on and live my life, and I will mind my own business." But this is not our option. In Deuteronomy 21 when an Israelite found someone slain lying in the field and it was not known who did it, the elders from the city closest to the field were required to go out into a valley and sacrifice a heifer. "And all the elders of that city, that are next unto the slain man, shall wash their hands over the heifer that is beheaded in the valley: and they shall answer and say, Our hands have not shed this blood, neither have our eyes seen it. Be merciful, O Lord, unto thy people Israel, whom thou hast redeemed, and lay not innocent blood unto thy people of Israel's charge. And the blood shall be forgiven them" (Deuteronomy 21:6-8).

Little do we understand that even today when a murder is committed and the murderer is not brought to justice, wrath is treasured up against the city. This is the reason for the sacrifice and for the plea for mercy in Israel. When innocent blood is shed, wrath is reserved for a day of destruction. This was Jeremiah's cry to his people: "Thus saith the Lord of hosts, the God of Israel; Behold, I will bring evil upon this place, the which whosoever heareth, his ear shall tingle. Because they have forsaken me, and have estranged this place, and have burned incense in it unto other gods, whom neither they nor their fathers have known, nor the kings of Judah, and have filled this place with the blood of innocents; they have built also the high places of Baal, to burn their sons with fire for burnt offerings unto Baal, which I commanded not, nor spake it, neither came it into my mind: therefore, behold, the days come, saith the Lord, that this place shall no more be called Tophet, nor The Valley of the son of Hinnom, but The Valley of slaughter" (Jeremiah 19:3b-6).

Our Decaying Society

What is happening in our cities across our nation is that we are treasuring up unto ourselves "wrath against the day of wrath and revelation of the righteous judgment of God" (Romans 2:5). It *is* of concern to us because, if the Lord tarry, it *shall* affect us greatly. We were willing to settle for a "no win" policy in Korea and so we settled for a "lose the war" policy in Viet Nam. The next step is to settle for "no contest" right here at home. We are already reaping the consequences of living high on the hog—way above our means—and we have just begun this process of reaping the results of such deficit spending. As a nation, whatever we do is wrong because we as a people are wrong spiritually and morally. We have forgotten that God takes the lid off of our cities, and what he sees is a stench to His nostrils. Nothing is hid from the eyes of Him with whom we have to do. We may well ask whether the celebration of our 200th anniversary would not better be described as the practice of our funeral. We somehow have the idea that God needs America, rather than the fact of the matter, that America needs God.

Available to us is the work of Edward Gibbon who, in 1787, after 20 years of labor, completed his *The Decline and Fall of the Roman Empire.* In it he attributed the fall of the Empire as being

1. "The rapid increase of divorce; the undermining of the dignity and sanctity of the home, which is the basis of human society."
2. "Higher and higher taxes and the spending of public monies for free bread and circuses for the populace."
3. "The mad craze for pleasure; sports becoming every year more exciting and more brutal."
4. "The building of gigantic armaments when the real enemy was within, the decadence of the people."
5. "The decay of religion—faith fading into mere form, losing touch with life and becoming impotent to warn and guide the people."

The "King's Business" magazine carried an article a few years ago that reported the average age of the world's great civilizations has been 200 years. These nations progressed through this sequence:

From Bondage to Spiritual Faith
From Spiritual Faith to Great Courage
From Courage to Liberty
From Liberty to Abundance
From Abundance to Selfishness
From Selfishness to Complacency
From Complacency to Apathy
From Apathy to Dependency
From Dependency back into Bondage.

You decide where you think we are in this schedule with our 200 years of existence.

An anonymous writer has written what is entitled, "The Hymn to the Welfare State." Listen to it and see if you think it may have any bearing upon the problems of today.

"The Government is my shepherd,
Therefore I need not work.
It alloweth me to lie down on a good job.
It leadeth me beside still factories;
It destroyeth my initiative.
It leadeth me in the path
    of a parasite for politic's sake.
Yea, though I walk through the valley of laziness and
    deficit-spending,
I will fear no evil, for the Government is with me.
It prepareth an economic Utopia for me, by appropri-
    ating the earnings of my own grandchildren.
It filleth my head with false security;
My inefficiency runneth over.
Surely the Government should care for me for all the
    days of my life!
And I shall dwell in a fool's paradise for ever."

Dr. Larry W. Poland calls our age "the irony age" and the reason is because "this is an age in which we can beam messages to the stars and yet our next door neighbors are going to eternity without the message of the Lord Jesus Christ. . . .

"It is an age in which we get all concerned about communism capturing the world, and we don't care that Satan is capturing our community.

"It is a time in which we have the greatest national defense in history of the world and the weakest moral defense.

"It is an age in which we'll pay five million dollars a year to a drunken television entertainer and five thousand dollars a year to a Bible College professor.

"It is an age in which we'll call a man a fan if he won't miss a ball game and a fanatic if he won't miss prayer meeting.

"It is a time when we'll imprison the man who is unfaithful to his debts and chuckle about the man who is unfaithful to his wife.

"It is a time in which we'll spend thousands training a machine gunner and practically nothing to train a minister of the Gospel."

The Art of Slow Approach

How have we come to this situation? We did it just one small step at a time. James M. Gray says: "There is on record a laboratory experiment in which a frog was placed in cool water being heated at a slow rate of .017 of a degree F. per second, and which, although it never moved, was found at the end of two and a half hours to be dead. The explanation was that at any point of time the temperature of water showed such a little contrast with that of a moment before that the attention of the frog was never attracted to it. It was boiled to death without noticing it!" So he continues: "Satan is a past master in the art of slow approach, taking his prey easily from things familiar to those that are unfamiliar. This sin and unbelief of today is not in marked contrast with that of yesterday. No shock is felt as men are drawn farther and farther away from God, and their attention is not permitted to rest upon it. The world will not know when it is ripe for judgment."

This was the very word of our Lord when He said: "But as the days of Noah were, so shall also the coming of the Son of man be. For as in the days that were before the flood they were eating and drinking, marrying and giving in marriage, until the day that Noah entered into the ark, and knew not until the flood came, and took them all away; so shall also the coming of the Son of man be" (Matthew 24:37-39). People were going on with life as usual until suddenly it was too late.

Daniel Webster warned us years ago: "If religious books are not widely circulated among the masses in this country and the people do not become religious, I do not know what is to become of us as a nation. And the thought is one to cause solemn reflection on the part of every patriot and Christian. If the truth be not diffused, error will be; if God and His Word are not known and received, the devil and his works will gain the ascendancy; if the evangelical volume does not reach every hamlet, the pages of corrupt and licentious literature will."

From the "Baptist Beacon" in the State of Illinois came the comment: "It is illegal to read the Bible in the public schools of Illinois, but a law requires the STATE to provide a Bible for every convict! Don't worry, kids, if you can't read the Bible in school, you'll be able to when you get to prison."

The Truth Still Stands

America has forgotten God, and we are reaping the results. It is as true today as when written that "Righteousness exalteth a nation: but sin is a reproach to any people" (Proverbs 14:34). Moreover, the Word clearly says, "Blessed is the nation whose God is the Lord" (Psalm 33:12); but our God today is not the Lord, nor are we trusting in Him. Our wealth, our armed strength, our technical skills are nothing but broken reeds without the Lord. Would to God we could say today that "some trust in chariots, and some in horses: but we will remember the name of the Lord our God" (Psalm 20:7).

It was at one time this way. J. A. Spencer wrote in his *History of the United States,* Volume 2, page 222, published in 1858, the following account that took place at the Federal Convention in July 1787 in Philadelphia. The several states were widely divided on the question of representation in Congress, the larger states being unwilling to allow smaller ones an equality in voting. It caused the Convention to be at a standstill. This occasioned Benjamin Franklin to say the following:

"Mr. President, the small progress we have made, after four or five weeks' close attendance and continual reasonings with each other, our different sentiments on almost every question, several of the last producing as many *noes* as *ayes,* is, methinks a melancholy proof of the imperfection of the human understanding. We indeed seem to feel our want of political wisdom, since we have been running all about in search of it. We have gone back to ancient history for models of government, and examined the different forms of those republics, which, having been originally formed with the seeds of their own dissolution, now no longer exist; and we have viewed modern states all around Europe, but find none of their constitutions suitable to our circumstances. In this situation of this Assembly, groping, as it were, in the dark, to find political truth, and scarce able to distinguish it when presented to us, how has it happened, Sir, that we have not hitherto once thought of humbly applying to the Father of Lights to illuminate our understandings? In the beginning of the contest with Britain, when we were sensible of danger, we had daily prayers in this room for the divine protection! Our prayers, Sir, were heard;—and they were graciously answered. All of us who were engaged in the struggle, must have observed frequent instances of a superintending providence in our favor.

"And have we now forgotten that powerful Friend? or

do we imagine we no longer need His assistance?

"I have lived, Sir, a long time; and the longer I live, the more convincing proofs I see of this truth, *That God governs in the affairs of men!* We have been assured, Sir, in the Sacred Writings, that 'except the Lord build the house, they labor in vain that build it!' I firmly believe this; and I also believe that without His concurring aid we shall succeed in this political building no better than the builders of Babel; we shall be divided by our little partial local interests, our projects will be confounded, and we ourselves shall become a reproach and a by-word down to future ages. And, what is worse, mankind may hereafter, from this unfortunate instance despair of establishing government by human wisdom, and leave it to chance, war and conquest.

"I therefore beg leave to move, that henceforth prayers, imploring the assistance of heaven, and its blessings on our deliberations, be held in this Assembly every morning and that one or more of the clergy of this city be requested to officiate in that service."

The Call for Vigilance

So it is today that God commands us that prayers "be made for all men; for kings, and for all that are in authority; that we may lead a quiet and peaceable life in all godliness and honesty" (1 Timothy 2:1-2). When our leaders sow wrong, we who are believers, right along with others, will be involved in reaping the wrong. We cannot escape the consequences of what happens in our midst. It is true that the righteous are spoken of both as salt and as light. As such the righteous have a preserving influence upon the wicked and God will not destroy the city if there are ten righteous in it. But let us never forget that the corrupt society also has a corrupting influence upon the good. Even Lot vexed his righteous soul day by day with the things he saw and heard in Sodom (2 Peter 2:7-8). Moreover, while Abraham was able to arm 318 servants, born in his own household, to fight against the victorious kings by faith because they had come to know Abraham's

God (Genesis 14:13-16), yet Lot, when he with his servants went down to Sodom, lost all of his servants to that godless society. Not one of his servants was saved when the cities of the plain were destroyed by God. Thus we can truthfully say a pattern is seen all through Scripture that evil and wickedness tend to increase more and more until judgment falls.

Indications of God's judgment are all around us if we would only observe what is going on. The main street to Anchorage, Fourth Avenue, was known as the mile-long bar, because, as we understand, it had more liquor establishments along it than any street of comparable size in any city of the world. In the earthquake that struck in 1964, this was the area that received the severest damage, and Fourth Avenue was almost entirely wiped out. Many of the folks remarked about the significance of the quake's striking *that location* on Good Friday.

When judgment has fallen upon this land, maybe someone will unearth the Lincoln Memorial and read the words quoted by Mr. Lincoln in his second inaugural address inscribed in stone: "The judgments of the Lord are true and righteous altogether."

We are and we will be reaping what others are sowing, and therefore it behooves us to do everything we can to stem the tide of lawlessness and wickedness, remembering that the only true solution is personal faith in the Lord Jesus Christ. Until a person has a new nature, being a new creation in Christ Jesus, he cannot live righteously. Therefore we do not need a reformed society, but a redeemed society. It does not do any good to wash a pig and put a big red ribbon around his neck. He is still a pig with a pig's nature, and when he has an opportunity he will go back to waddling in the mire. Until his nature is changed, his actions cannot permanently change.

Whenever God sent blights, draughts and plagues upon the people of Israel, the prophets cried out to the Nation: "This is from God" (cf. Joel 1:1-12; Amos 4:6-11). God's indictment leveled against Israel was "yet have ye not returned unto me, saith the Lord." Can He who made the earth and the fullness thereof use these means today or have we become educated beyond intelligence? Not a year goes by that we are not experiencing a draught in one place, flooding in another and blight in another to say nothing of hurricane, tornado and earthquake destruction. If you don't believe it, watch it happen!

If the Word is true—"Blessed is that nation whose God is the Lord" (Psalm 33:12)—then it follows axiomatically that any nation whose God is not the Lord will not be blessed. But another principle found throughout the Word is that light creates responsibility. "For unto whomsoever much is given, of him shall be much required" (cf. Luke 12:47-48). It is one thing not to know the Lord; it is another thing not to obey Him; but it is worse yet to turn away from Him in rebellion. As the cry of the prophets fell upon deaf ears to a former Nation, so it seems that we are repeating today the words voiced by another: "Who is the Lord, that I should obey his voice" (Exodus 5:2). In doing this we need to be prepared for the full demonstration of His power . . . in judgment.

2

IDENTIFYING

LAW #2   WE REAP THE SAME IN KIND AS WE SOW.

Had anyone spoken to David right after his involvement with Bathsheba (2 Samuel 11), and said, "David, before you are through, you will have broken every commandment of the Lord on the second table of the Law," without question he would have replied most emphatically, "Man, you must be crazy. I would *never* do anything like that!"

But he did! He committed murder (2 Samuel 11:15), adultery (11:4); he stole (11:4); he bore false witness (11:8, 21); as well as coveting his neighbor's wife (11:2, 3). Here, vividly portrayed, is the deceitfulness of sin (Hebrews 3:13) which is one of the reasons we are to exhort one another daily because sin has such a hardening affect upon a life.

But as bad as this was, it was just the beginning, for every one of these sins was to be reaped within his own family. Thus may be seen a very important law of the harvest.

LAW #2. WE REAP THE SAME IN KIND AS WE SOW.

In the six days of creation, God ordered everything to produce "after his kind." Notice that three times in Genesis 1:11 and 12 this is emphasized. "And God said, Let the earth bring forth grass, the herb yielding seed, and the fruit tree yielding fruit *after his kind,* whose seed is in itself, upon the earth: and it was so. And the earth brought forth grass, and herb yielding seed *after his kind,* and the tree yielding fruit, whose seed was in itself, *after his kind:* and God saw that it was good." What is true in the botanical realm is also true in the zoological realm, so that the entire realm of biology is governed in the natural sphere by this law (cf. Genesis 1:20-22, 24-25 where "after his [their] kind" is repeated seven more times).

The Use of This Law with Nicodemus

So abiding is this law that our Lord used it when speaking to Nicodemus. He said: "That which is born of the flesh is flesh; and that which is born of the Spirit is spirit" (John 3:6). All that the flesh is capable of producing is like in kind as itself—more flesh. Likewise, the Holy Spirit of God reproduces after His own holy nature and character and produces a new nature within the believer. This is His work which we call regeneration.

Titus 3:5 says: "Not by works of righteousness which we have done, but according to his mercy he saved us, by the washing of regeneration, and renewing of the Holy Spirit." "Regeneration" is a composite of two words in the Greek language. The first word signifies "again," "once more," and the second word is the word for "birth," "creation." Thus regeneration is a "once more birth"; it is a "creation all over again." Being born once will never fit us for heaven; we must be born all over again by the Holy Spirit of God. But it is a different kind of a birth than our first birth; it is a spiritual birth. It is this very thing that is the heart of Christianity. The Spirit's work of regeneration is to take our personality and to equip it to live in God's presence forever. This is why the Lord said to Nicodemus: "Marvel not that I said unto thee, Ye must be born again" (John 3:7).

Think, if you will, of the implication of this statement. Here was Nicodemus, a man who had everything going for him. He was educated, socially prominent, *very* religious; for, being a Pharisee, he was more religious than any among us today. (Pharisees would fast twice a week, on Mondays and Thursdays, and were meticulously scrupulous about principles that governed every aspect of their lives.) Here was someone morally upright and outstanding in every way, being a member of the Sanhedrin in Jerusalem—the highest ruling body in Israel. He was the type of person that any mother in Israel would have been glad to say to her child: "Son, when you grow up, I trust you will be as outstanding and good as Nicodemus." Yet even though he was that kind of person, our Lord said to him that he had to be born again to see the kingdom of God. *He could not make it on his own merit.*

Now later on in the next chapter of John's Gospel, our Lord is talking to a woman at the well at Sychar in Samaria. She was a Samaritan, a mixture of Jew and Gentile—a person despised and detested by every Israelite. She was an outcast as far as the Jews were concerned, for the Jews had "no dealings with the Samaritans" (John 4:9). The degree of animosity between Jews and Samaritans may be seen in the fact that the Jews felt Gentiles, whom they called "dogs," could be saved by becoming proselytes and coming within Judaism. But their teaching, according to Edersheim, was that it was an impossibility for any Samaritans to be saved and enter the Kingdom. They were without hope. This attitude only deepened the bitter feelings between Samaritans and Jews.

Now, even in Samaria, this woman was a notorious person; for the Lord Jesus exposes to her that He knew she had had five husbands and was now living with a man she had never married. But the point that needs to be seen is that our Lord never spoke one word to this Samaritan woman about being born again, but rather spoke about the Father, and the loving heart of the Father who desires "true worshippers" (John 4:21-24). Why did He not speak to her about the new birth? Very simply, because had the

Lord spoken to her about being born again we would all have said, "Yes, she needs to be born anew because of her bad background and state. *But we were not born like that;* therefore, we do not need to be born again. We are acceptable as we are." However, since the Lord chose the very best specimen in Israel, Nicodemus, and said to him, "Ye must be born again," all of us, without exception, must be born again in order to see the kingdom of God. If the very best in Israel could not make it on his own, no one else could who did not come up to Nicodemus' human standard of excellence.

What the Lord is teaching here is identical with what Paul taught later on, namely, we have all fallen short of the glory of God (Romans 3:23). Some of us may have fallen short more than others, but not one of us can make it on his own. In order to have a nature in like kind with God, we must be born again; we must be born from above. There are no exceptions.

The Absoluteness of This Law

Since everything reproduces after its kind, God will never be mocked. No one will ever sow sweet peas and reap cucumbers. Neither can anyone sow that which is wrong and reap that which is right. Paul stresses this fact in Galatians 6. "Be not deceived; God is not mocked: for whatsoever a man soweth, that shall he also reap. For he that soweth to his flesh shall of the flesh reap corruption; but he that soweth to the Spirit shall of the Spirit reap life everlasting" (vv. 7-8). Paul's warning is given to those who are believers since only the believer has the Holy Spirit and a spiritual nature, and can therefore, sow to the Spirit. Since everything reproduces after its kind, we do not sow discord and reap unity; we do not sow sin and reap sanctification; we do not sow hypocrisy and reap holiness of life. He who sows to his flesh will reap just what the flesh can produce. But he that sows to the Spirit will reap what the Spirit can produce. Even Eliphaz in the book of Job recognized this abiding principle, when he exclaimed:

". . .they that plow iniquity, and sow wickedness, reap the same" (Job 4:8).

When David sowed to the flesh, he reaped what the flesh produced. Moreover, he reaped the consequences of his actions even though he had confessed his sin and been forgiven for it. Underline it, star it, mark it deeply upon your conscious mind: *Confession and forgiveness in no way stop the harvest.* He had sown; he was to reap. Forgiven he was, but the consequences continued. This is exactly the emphasis Paul is giving the Galatians even in this age of grace. We are not to be deceived for God will not be mocked. What we sow we will reap, and there are *no exceptions.*

Now to err is human, for as Solomon said, "There is not a just man upon earth, that doeth good, and sinneth not" (Ecclesiastes 7:20). But to remain in error is stupid. The sooner we stop sowing to the flesh, the sooner we will stop reaping the harvest. Had David only sinned with Bathsheba, his sin would have been great enough; but David kept on and on in his sin until finally he killed Uriah. Since he had sown the more, he was to reap the more. To state this principle negatively, every kick has a kickback; yet each new generation has to learn it all over again.

The Effect Upon Our Children

Much of our sowing and reaping is involved with that of our children. This was where David was to reap the consequences of his actions; and this, likewise, governs much of our sowing and reaping because children are so impressionable and pick up even our unconscious attitudes, to say nothing of seeing and imitating our actions. Many a time I have been unaware of my own attitude or action until I had it mirrored back to me in my son or daughter.

I wish every one of us had inscribed on the walls of our home the words of Dorothy Law Nolte's work, "Children Learn What They Live," and then kept this constantly before us in our daily activities.

If a child lives with criticism,
  HE learns to condemn.
If a child lives with hostility,
  HE learns to fight.
If a child lives with ridicule,
  HE learns to be shy.
If a child lives with shame,
  HE learns to feel guilty.
If a child lives with tolerance,
  HE learns to be patient.
If a child lives with encouragement,
  HE learns confidence.
If a child lives with praise,
  HE learns to appreciate.
If a child lives with fairness,
  HE learns justice.
If a child lives with security,
  HE learns to have faith.
If a child lives with approval,
  HE learns to like himself.
If a child lives with acceptance and friendship,
  HE learns to find love in the world.

Oh, if we only realized even in a small degree that our actions speak louder than our words. I was in a home in another state for two days where the parents said they loved the Lord sincerely; and, if you would have asked them, they would have said that they would desire nothing better than that their three children would serve the Lord Jesus Christ when they grew up. Yet for the two days I was there in that home I sought at every meal to turn the conversation to the Word of God and the Lord Jesus Christ. Not one time in the six meals did I succeed. Today not one of those children who are now grown cares anything about the Lord and never attends church. The seed was deeply sown, but, unfortunately, it was the wrong seed.

Several years ago, "Our Daily Bread" carried an article by an anonymous author on the power of example. It would be worth our repeating it here.

"One day when Junior was 14 he noticed his father wearing a happy grin as he came home from the office.

" 'Got pinched for speeding, but Jake down at the city hall got the ticket fixed for me,' he said.

"When Junior was 15, he was with his mother in the family car when she backed into a tree. The damage would easily exceed $100.

" 'We'll say someone rammed into us when we were parked downtown,' she said. 'Then we'll collect insurance for it.'

"When the boy was 16, he listened to his grandfather reminiscing about the 'good old days of rationing' when he made $100,000 black-marketing cars. That same night Uncle John was bragging that on a good share of his business he sent no bills and took no checks—just cash.

" 'Why be a sucker and let those punks in the Internal Revenue Department get all my money?' he asked.

"When Junior turned 18, his family pulled every possible string to get him a paid scholarship at a coveted Ivy League school. They even lied about the family income to make it seem that their son needed financial aid. When he had a rough time scholastically, an upperclassman sold him the answers to the calculus examination. Junior was caught and expelled. When he returned home, his mother burst into hysterical weeping over the disgrace he had caused.

" 'How could you have done this to us'; she sobbed. 'This isn't the way we raised you.' "

I have a feeling I know why this was written anonymously; it is too like the real thing not to be based upon reality. As someone has well expressed it: "As the twig is bent, it is apt to snap back in your face."

But we should not just think negatively in this area of sowing and reaping, but rather consider the positive example. As a parent what can you do that will enable.you to

be the greatest possible influence you can to your child?
Here are some positive steps.

1. Make home the brightest and most attractive place on
    earth. Make it a little bit of heaven where the fruit of
    the Spirit of love, joy, peace, longsuffering, gentleness,
    goodness, faithfulness, meekness and self-control are
    seen in your life.

2. Let your child invite his friends to your home and
    table so that he would rather be home than anywhere
    else on earth. In order to accomplish this, have a good
    sense of humor and do things together as a family.

3. Make him responsible for the performance of a certain
    limited number of daily duties. Thus, never do for
    your child what he is capable of doing for himself or
    else you will make him a dependent cripple.

4. Never punish him in anger; and, when he is to be
    punished, seek to punish him only in the degree and
    the way that the Lord punishes you.

5. Talk about the Lord and the Word, not as something
    foreign to life and its activities, but as the natural
    outflow of your life as a family so that the Lord is
    seen as the very heart and center of all your thoughts
    and actions.

6. Do not criticize your child as a person, but rather
    encourage his abilities and help him over his weak-
    nesses and discouragements. Be generous with your
    praise. Laugh, yes, but only at *your* mistakes. Never
    tease. It is meanness.

7. Live uprightly before him at all times, but do not
    hesitate to confess your weaknesses and ask forgive-
    ness of him when you fail. It is very hard for a child
    to confess a mistake if he has never had the example.

8. Let him hear, "I love you," not only to your wife,
    but also to him; and then show it by treating him
    with respect. He wants this more than anything else.

9. Be careful to impress upon his mind that making

character is more important than making money, and prove it to him by your seeking to improve yourself as a person.
10. Be much in prayer that the Lord would overrule your mistakes and work in accordance with the very intent of your heart. A contrite and humble heart before God accomplishes much.

These are surely not all the things that might be done by us who are parents for you can go on and add another ten items to these, but here is at least a start.

One of the great statesman of the past generation wrote this prayer to God for his son. You might want to pray something like this yourself as you seek to sow that which is positive in his life.

"Build me a son, O Lord, who will be strong enough to know when he is weak—and brave enough to face himself when he is afraid. One who will be proud and unbending in honest defeat, but humble and gentle in victory.

"Build me a son whose wishes will not replace his actions, a son who will know Thee, and that to know himself is the foundation stone of knowledge.

"Send him, I pray, not in the path of ease and comfort but in the street and spur of difficulties and challenge. Here let him learn to stand up in the storm; here let him learn compassion for those who fail. Build me a son whose heart will be clear, whose goal will be high—a son who will master himself before he seeks to master others.

"One who will learn to laugh, yet never forget how to weep; one who will reach into the future; yet never forget the past.

"And after all of these things are his—this I pray—enough sense of humor that he may always be serious; yet never take himself too seriously.

"Give him humility so that he may always remember the simplicity of true greatness, the open mind of true wisdom, the meekness of true strength.

"Then I, his father, will dare to whisper, 'I have not lived in vain.' "

This prayer was written by General Douglas Mac-Arthur.

We Can Affect The Reactions of Others

From a study of this law of the harvest, perhaps we can begin to realize that our own soul is but a mirror of what will come back to us. "A soft answer turneth away wrath: but grievous words stir up anger" (Proverbs 15:1). A man with a calmness within can create a calmness without, while another with turmoil within sows contention without.

The "Sunday School Times" carried a story many years ago that I have never forgotten that conveyed something of this idea in it.

"One day a mover's wagon came past Farmer Jones' gate. Farmer Jones was friendly to everybody, so he asked the movers where they were going.

" 'We are moving from Johnstown to Jamestown,' they told him. 'Can you tell us what kind of neighbors we will find there?'

" 'What kind did you find in Johnstown?'

" 'The very worst kind,' they said. 'Gossipy, unkind, and indifferent. We are glad to move away.'

" 'You will find the same in Jamestown.'

The next day another mover's wagon passed, and similar conversation took place. The second party asked what neighbors they would find in Johnstown and were asked what kind they had found in Jamestown.

" 'The very best. So kind and considerate, it almost broke our hearts to move away.'

" 'You will find exactly the same kind in Johnstown,' was the farmer's reply."

This second law of the harvest is that we reap the same in kind as we sow. It is not the same, but the same in kind. This is Paul's argument in 1 Corinthians 15 where he stresses there is a correspondence between what is sown and what is reaped (cf. vv. 42, 44). But the fact remains, although not always indentical, when we lie to others, others will ultimately lie to us. If we cheat others, someday someone will cheat us. As the writer of Ecclesiastes has well said it: "He that diggeth a pit shall fall into it." (Ecclesiastes 10:8). The one who digs a pit to trap others will surely fall into it himself. This is God's law of retribution. Many passages throughout Scripture speak of this same truth (cf. Psalms 7:15-16; 9:15-16; 10:2; 35:7-8; 37:14-15; 57:6; Proverbs 26:27). Scripture, furthermore, abounds with examples of this principle. "They hanged Haman on the gallows that he had prepared for Mordecai" (Esther 7:10). Jacob schemed to get the blessing due to the firstborn, and Laban later tricked him with the rights of the firstborn (Genesis 29:20-26). Just as Jacob lied, so someone lied to him. As he plotted against someone else, someone else plotted against him. So, likewise, even as Paul caused great suffering for Christians, he himself was to suffer greatly for the Gospel of Christ (Acts 9:16; 2 Corinthians 11:23-27). I do not feel that it is an accident that Paul was the one responsible for Stephen's being stoned to death (Acts 7:58); and then later on, Paul was stoned and left for dead himself (Acts 14:19).

Paul knew too well the absoluteness of this law of the harvest, and it is on this basis that he solemnly warns the Galatian believers: "Be not deceived; God is not mocked: for whatsoever a man soweth that shall he also reap. For he that soweth to his flesh shall of the flesh reap corruption; but he that soweth to the Spirit shall of the Spirit reap life everlasting" (Galatians 6:7-8).

3

WAITING

LAW #3   WE REAP IN A DIFFERENT SEASON THAN
WHEN WE SOW.

Too many believers are sowing wild oats through the week and then going to church on Sunday and praying for a crop failure. But it will not happen, for God will not be mocked by man—any man. Even though we may scheme and connive and try to get around reaping the consequences of our actions, our puny efforts are like trying to stop a forest fire with a toy water pistol or a plague of locusts with an aerosol bomb of bug spray. It shall not be done. The laws of the harvest abide.

What you sow you will reap. When you sow good, you reap the good, but when you sow the wrong you reap the same in kind. Psalm 7:15 and 16 reads: "He made a pit, and digged it, and is fallen into the ditch which he made. His mischief shall return upon his own head, and his violent dealing shall come down upon his own pate." Psalm 9:16 states: "The Lord is known by the judgment which he executeth: the wicked is snared in the work of his own hands." God's fixed law is that "whoso diggeth a pit shall fall therein: and he that rolleth a stone, it will return upon him" (Proverbs 26:27). What you do to hurt others will come back upon yourself.

But this is not just a negative principle, for the Word stresses that it operates positively as well. The writer of Ecclesiastes says: "Cast thy bread upon the waters: for thou shalt find it after many days" (Ecclesiastes 11:1). Moreover, it is on the basis of the positive aspect of this principle that the Apostle Paul exhorts the Galatians to sow the good by means of the Spirit of God and, having done that, to "let us not be weary in well doing: for in due season we shall reap, if we faint not" (Galatians 6:9).

Now these verses open up before us a very important third abiding fact in the laws of the harvest, and it is this.

LAW #3. WE REAP IN A DIFFERENT SEASON THAN WHEN WE SOW.

The harvest never comes immediately after planting; for, while the earth abides, there is seedtime and harvest, cold and heat, summer and winter. These shall not cease (Genesis 8:22). There is a time when you plant and there is a time when you harvest, but these are not the same time. The harvest comes in a different season from the planting of the seed. This is just as true spiritually as it is physically; it is just as abiding for each and every person on this earth, as it is for the farmer who tills the ground. Also it is equally true whether you sow that which is bad or that which is good. Whatever is sown is not reaped immediately. The harvest comes in God's time—His appointed season.

The Positive Aspects of the Law

Again quoting Ecclesiastes 11:1, "Cast thy bread upon the waters: for thou shalt find it after many days." By the very fact that Solomon uses "bread" and not "grain," he shows this is a figure of speech; it is figurative language. Some feel that the imagery involves the custom in Egypt of casting the seed upon the face of the waters from boats when the Nile was in flood stage. Then when the waters receded, the grain germinated in the rich soil. Yet Solomon does not refer to casting grain upon the waters, but bread. Others have felt that this custom would not have been familiar in Israel, and that the picture employed refers to Solomon's sending forth upon the waters cargo vessels that left every three years with supplies and returned with "gold, silver, ivory" and the treasures of the nations (1 Kings 10:22; cf. Proverbs 31:14).

While the truth is in pictorial language, the principle is clear. Do deeds of kindness and they will later return to you again in accordance with the laws of sowing and reaping. They will come back to you like in kind; they will come in accordance with the principle of the harvest, namely at a different season from the sowing. It will be "after many days" (Ecclesiastes 11:1). Paul refers to this as "due season." "And let us not be weary in well doing: for in due season we shall reap, if we faint not" (Galatians 6:9). It is for this reason we are to do good, as we have opportunity, unto all (Galatians 6:10). Proverbs 11:18 says, "But to him that soweth righteousness shall be a sure reward." God is debtor to no man. The righteous shall reap a good, full harvest; this is His promise.

The entire Epistle of Titus was written to believers that they "be careful to maintain good works" (cf. 1:16; 2:7; 3:1, 8, 14). Even though we are not saved by good works (Titus 3:5; Ephesians 2:8-9), we are saved unto good works, and we are to "walk in them" (Ephesians 2:10). As Solomon penned it: "In the morning sow thy seed, and in the evening withhold not thine hand: for thou knowest not whether shall prosper, either this or that, or whether they both shall be alike good" (Ecclesiastes 11:6). The message, then, is that we are to sow all the good we can, doing everything we have opportunity to do, and leave the results with God. He is the One who gives the increase, and we really do not know whether He will bless one thing or another that we do, or whether He might bless it all and give us a bountiful harvest of good.

> I have wept in the night
> For the shortness of sight,
> That to somebody's need made me blind:
> But I never have yet

Felt a twinge of regret,
For being a little too kind.

—Anonymous

The Negative Aspects of the Law

The story is told of a farmer who prided himself in working his farm on Sunday and taunted his neighbor who was a Christian for not plowing and working then too.

"You just wait," he exclaimed, "for when harvest time comes I will have even better a harvest than yours. Your resting on Sunday and going to church will not help you one bit."

The summer passed and the harvest came, and from all outward appearance the man's harvest had a slightly better yield per acre.

Then the unbelieving farmer said to his Christian neighbor: "What do you have to say about that, neighbor?"

"Just one word, sir. God doesn't settle all His accounts in September!"

Oh, let us never forget it. Sometimes the Lord in His longsuffering waits years before He disciplines or judges for wrongs. When the Israelites were in the land, they failed to keep the Sabbatical year during which time no one in Israel was to work the land or plant anything. For a whole year, each seventh year, the land was to rest (Exodus 23:10-11; Leviticus 25:1-7; Deuteronomy 15:1; 31:10). Yet for a period of 490 years (whether intermittently or consecutively we do not know) Israel failed to observe this injunction. It may have appeared at first that it made no difference, that God wasn't noticing it at all; but this was the furthest thing from the truth. He waited and waited, and then after nearly half a millennium He told the people that they were going off the land for 70 years (Jeremiah 25:11-12; 29:10), and at the end of that time they were to return. The reason for the 70 years was so the land could enjoy and keep its sabbaths that the people had failed to observe (Leviticus 26:33, 34, 43; 2 Chronicles 36:21). All the time God had been keeping an exact account.

Solomon in Ecclesiastes had the wisdom to state the nature of the situation accurately when he wrote, "Because sentence against an evil work is not executed speedily, therefore the heart of the sons of men is fully set in them to do evil" (Ecclesiastes 8:11). Because God does not judge sin instantly, men think they are getting by with sinning, while in reality they are not getting by with anything. They may postulate the proposition that "God is dead" or He is on a vacation and is not involved in the affairs of this life, but all they are doing is showing their ignorance indeed. "Behold, he that keepeth Israel shall neither slumber nor sleep" (Psalm 121:4). "Hast thou not known? hast thou not heard, that the everlasting God, the Lord, the Creator of the ends of the earth, fainteth not, neither is weary; there is no searching of his understanding" (Isaiah 40:28).

Sometimes the cup of iniquity is full and the people ripe for judgment. In such a case it may happen as it did in the flourishing and extraordinarily beautiful city of Messina, Italy. In the early morning of December 28, 1908, an earthquake struck, and 84,000 human beings died. We read, as reported in the "Evangelical Christian": "Only a few hours before that devastating earthquake which laid Messina and the surrounding districts in ruins, the unspeakable wicked and irreligious condition of some of the inhabitants was expressed in a series of violent resolutions which were passed against all religious principles, while the journal 'Il Telefono,' printed in Messina, actually published in its Christmas number an abominable parody, daring the Almightly to make Himself known by sending an earthquake! And in three days the earthquake came!" (Quoted by Dr. Louis S. Bauman in the "Sunday School Times").

The "Earnest Worker" has quoted S. D. Gordon as saying, "There are seven important things we ought always to remember about sin. The first is that "sin earns wages." The second, "sin pays wages." The third, "sin insists on paying. You may be quite willing to let the account go, but sin always insists on paying." Fourth, "sin pays its wages in kind. Sin against the body brings results in the body. Sin in the moral life brings results there. Sin in contact with other people brings a chain of results affecting those others. Sin is the most selfish of acts. It influences to some extent everything we touch." Fifth, "sin pays in installments." Sixth, "sin pays in full, unless the blood of Jesus washes away the stain." Seventh, "sin is self-executive, it pays its own bills. Sin has bound up in itself all the terrible consequences that ever come."

No wonder the Word so strongly admonishes: "My son, if sinners entice thee, consent thou not" (Proverbs 1:10). As Charles H. Spurgeon so well expressed it: "Put your foot down where you mean to stand, and let no man move you from the right. Learn to say 'No,' and it will be of more use to you than to be able to read Latin."

Two Ways—Two Destinies

Our Lord said there are but two ways to travel life: "Enter ye in at the strait gate: for wide is the gate, and broad is the way, that leadeth to destruction, and many there be which go in thereat: because strait is the gate, and narrow is the way, which leadeth unto life, and few there be that find it" (Matthew 7:13-14). Here we have two gates. The narrow gate is the person and work of the Lord Jesus Christ; the broad gate is the teaching that there are many religious beliefs and they all contain some truth. Here we have two ways, and these two ways are opposite the one from the other. The straight way is the way revealed in the Word of God alone, while the broad way is that which men have constructed in human philosophies and ideas. The two destinies are final destinies. One is life and the other is destruction. The division of mankind is divided over the many who are traveling the wrong way to destruction and the few that are going the way to life eternal. Each person is either heading one direction or another. He has either entered the narrow gate of the cross work of Jesus Christ that leads into the greatness of life in all of its abundance and fullness, or else he is traveling the broad road with the multitude that is heading for the blackness of darkness forever. This is why our Lord said: "If therefore the light that is within thee be darkness, how great is that darkness" (Matthew 6:23). The person who is unsaved is in darkness and continues in more darkness, while the Word stresses that "the path of the just is as the shining light, that shineth more and more unto the perfect day" (Proverbs 4:18). Both are the products of sowing and reaping. The believer sows light and reaps greater light; the unbeliever sows darkness and stumbles all the more in the darkness that blinds his mind and heart.

The contrast is not seen anywhere more vividly than that which exists between two poems which Dr. Alva J. McClain, former President of Grace Theological Seminary, gave in his theology class notes. The one is entitled, "Invictus" written by William E. Henley, who, by the way, died of suicide. The other is written by a believer in the Lord Jesus Christ, Dorothea Day, and her poem is entitled, "My Captain." Observe, if you will, the difference in them.

INVICTUS
Out of the night that covers me,
    Black as the pit from pole to pole,
I thank whatever gods may be
    For my unconquerable soul.

In the fell clutch of circumstance
    I have not winced nor cried aloud.
Under the bludgeonings of chance
    My head is bloody, but unbowed.

Beyond this place of wrath and tears
    Looms but the horror of the shade,
And yet the menace of the years
    Finds and shall find me unafraid.

It matters not how strait the gate,
    How charged with punishments the scroll,
I am the master of my fate:
    I am the captain of my soul.

MY CAPTAIN

Out of the light that dazzles me,
    Bright as the sun from pole to pole,
I thank the God I know to be
    For Christ the conqueror of my soul.

Since His the sway of circumstance,
    I would not wince nor cry aloud.
Under that rule which men call chance
    My head with joy is humbly bowed.

Beyond this place of sin and tears
    That life with Him! And His the aid,
Despite the menace of the years,
    Keeps, and shall keep me, unafraid.

I have no fear, though strait the gate,
    He cleared from punishment the scroll.
Christ is the Master of my fate,
    Christ is the Captain of my soul.

Dying Statements of the Unsaved

Listen to the difference in the recorded testimonies of those who died without Christ and those who died with Him. First are those who sowed their lives against the Lord Jesus Christ and the truth of the Word of God, and here is what they reaped in death.

Talleyrand Perigord: "I am suffering the pangs of the damned."

Merabeau: "Give me laudanum that I may not think of eternity."

Francis Newport: "Oh, that I was to lie a thousand

years upon the fire that never is quenched, to purchase the favor of God, and be united to Him again! But it is a fruitless wish. Millions of millions of years would bring me no nearer to the end of my torments than one poor hour. Oh, eternity, eternity! forever and forever! Oh, the insufferable pangs of hell!"

Thomas Hobbs: a skeptic: "If I had the whole world, I would give it to live one day. I shall be glad to find a hole to creep out of the world at. About to take a leap into the dark!"

Thomas Paine: the noted American infidel and author: "I would give worlds if I had them, that *The Age of Reason* had never been published. O Lord, help me! Christ, help me! O God, what have I done to suffer so much? But there is no God! But if there should be, what will become of me hereafter? Stay with me, for God's sake! Send even a child to stay with me, for it is hell to be alone. If ever the Devil had an agent, I have been that one."

Francois Voltaire: the noted French infidel. He was one of the most fertile and talented writers and strove to retard and demolish Christianity. His cry in health concerning Christ was, "Curse the wretch!" He said once, "In twenty years, Christianity will be no more. My single hand shall destroy the edifice it took twelve apostles to rear." Some years after his death, his very printing press was employed in printing New Testaments.

The Christian physician who attended Voltaire during the last illness, has left a testimony concerning the departure of this poor lost soul. He wrote to a friend as follows: "When I compare the death of a righteous man, which is like the close of a beautiful day, with that of Voltaire, I see the difference between bright, serene weather and a black thunderstorm. It was my lot that this man should die under my hands. Often did I tell him the truth.

'Yes, my friend,' he would often say to me, 'you are the only one who has given me good advice. Had I but followed it I would not be in the horrible condition in which I now am. I have swallowed nothing but smoke. I have intoxicated myself with the incense that turned my head. You can do nothing for me. Send me a mad doctor! Have compassion on me—I am mad!' "

The physician goes on to say: "I cannot think of it without shuddering. As soon as he saw that all the means he had employed to increase his strength had just the opposite effect, death was constantly before his eyes. From this moment, madness took possession of his soul. He expired under the torments of the furies."

At another time his doctor quoted Voltaire as saying: "I am abandoned by God and man! I will give you half of what I am worth if you will give me six months' life. Then I shall go to hell; and you will go with me. O Christ! O Jesus Christ!"

Charles IX: This cruel wretch, urged on by his inhumane mother, gave the order for the massacre of the Huguenots in which 15,000 souls were slaughtered in Paris alone, and 100,000 in other sections of France, for no other reason than that they owned Christ as their master. The guilty King died bathed in blood bursting from his own veins. To his physicians he said in his last hours: "Asleep or awake, I see the mangled forms of the Huguenots passing before me. They drip with blood. They point at their open wounds. Oh! that I had spared at least the little infants at the breast! What blood! I know not where I am. How will all this end? What shall I do? I am lost forever! I know it. Oh, I have done wrong. God pardon me!"

David Strauss: outstanding representative of German rationalism, after spending years of his life trying to dispense with God: "My philosophy leaves me utterly forlorn! I feel like one caught in the merciless jaws of an automatic machine, not knowing at what time one of its great hammers may crush me!"

Sir Thomas Scott: "Until this moment I thought there was neither a God nor a hell. Now I *know* and *feel* that there are both, and I am doomed to perdition by the just judgment of the Almighty."

M. F. Rich: an atheist: "I would rather lie on a stove and broil for a million years than go into eternity with eternal horrors that hang over my soul! I have given my immortality for gold; and its weight sinks me into an endless, hopeless, helpless hell."

Dying Statements of the Saved

Now let us take the contrast. Here are believers in the Lord Jesus Christ who have accepted the grace of God for salvation for both time and eternity.

Jordan Antie: "The chariot has come, and I am ready to step in."

Margaret Prior: "Eternity rolls up before me like a sea of glory."

Martha McCrackin: "How bright the room! How full of angels."

Dr. Cullen: "I wish I had the power of writing: I would describe how pleasant it is to die."

B. S. Bangs: "The sun is setting: mine is rising. I go from this bed to a crown. Farewell."

John Arthur Lyth: "Can this be death? Why, it is better than living! Tell them I die happy in Jesus."

Trotter: "I am in perfect peace, resting alone on the blood of Christ. I find this amply sufficient with which to enter the presence of God."

Mrs. Mary Frances: "Oh, that I could tell you what joy I possess! I am full of rapture. The Lord doth shine with such power upon my soul. He is come! He is come!

Philip Heck: "How beautiful! The opening heavens around me shine!"

Sir David Brewster: inventor of the kaleidoscope: "I will see Jesus: I shall see Him as He is. I have had the light for many years. Oh, how bright it is! I feel so safe and satisfied!"

Charles Wesley: author of over 4,000 published hymns: "I shall be satisfied with Thy likeness. Satisfied!"

John Wesley: "The best of all is, God is with me."

Abbott: "Glory to God! I see heaven sweetly opened before me."

Augustus Toplady: author of "Rock of Ages": "The consolations of God to such an unworthy wretch are so abundant that He leaves me nothing to pray for but a continuance of them. I enjoy heaven already in my soul."

John Quincy Adams: When John Quincy Adams was eighty years of age a friend said to him: "Well, how is John Quincy Adams?" "Thank you," he said, "John Quincy Adams is quite well. But the house where he lives is becoming dilapidated. It is tottering. Time and the seasons have nearly destroyed it, and it is becoming quite uninhabitable. I shall have to move out soon. But John Quincy Adams is quite well, thank you." At death he said: "This is the last of earth. I am content."

Mrs. Catherine Booth: wife of the general of the Salvation Army: "The waters are rising, but so am I. I am not going under, but over. Do not be concerned about dying; go on living well, the dying will be right."

Elizabeth B. Browning: an English poetess who had said: "We want the touch of Christ's hand upon our literature." At death's door, she said: "It is beautiful!"

John Bunyan: author of *Pilgrim's Progress*: "Weep not for me, but for yourselves. I go to the Father of our Lord Jesus Christ, who will, through the mediation of His blessed Son, receive me, though a sinner, where I hope we shall meet to sing the new song, and remain everlastingly happy, world without end."

John Calvin: the French Protestant Reformer at Geneva: "Thou, Lord, bruisest me, but I am abundantly satisfied, since it is from Thy hand."

Adoniram Judson: American missionary to Burma. He wrote: "Come, Holy Spirit, Dove Divine," and other hymns. He died at sea and his body was committed to the great deep. He said: "I go with the gladness of a boy bounding away from school. I feel so strong in Christ."

A. J. Gordon: As he lay in the chamber in West Brookline Street, Boston, looked up and with one radiant burst of joy cried: "Victory! Victory!" and so he went home.

Dr. William Anderson: of Dallas, Texas: He seemed better though still very ill. His mother was sitting in the room with him. He gently called to her, "Come over here a minute." As she approached his bed, he said, "I want to tell you something. I am going to beat you to heaven." And with a smile he shut his eyes and was gone.

Dr. Sewall: an old Methodist, when dying shouted aloud the praises of God. His friends said, "Dr. Sewall, do not exert yourself; whisper, doctor, whisper." "Let angels whisper," said he, "but the soul cleansed from sin by the blood of Christ, a soul redeemd from death and hell, just on the threshold of eternal glory—oh, if I had a voice that would reach from pole to pole, I would proclaim it to all the world: Victory! Victory! through the blood of the Lamb!"

Samuel Rutherford: When he was dying said: "I am in the happiest pass to which man ever came. Christ is mine, and I am His; and there is nothing now between me and resurrection, except—Paradise."

When you die, on which side of the ledger will your words be?

4

REMEMBERING

LAW #4   WE REAP MORE THAN WE SOW.

The fourth law of the harvest is one of the most important aspects concerning the harvest that there is. If it were not for this fact, there would be no harvest: and yet this is not something preached or seen in print. This is all the more amazing when you consider it is so simple.

LAW #4. WE REAP MORE THAN WE SOW.

If it were not for this abiding fact in the process of sowing and reaping, no farmer would plant anything. If he only got back what germinated in the ground, he would be on the losing end of the process since some seed falls upon the hard path and is lost to the birds of the air. Some seed is lost because it falls where there is not enough depth of ground to support life; and still other plants that grow are choked out by the dominance of thorn bushes and so never reproduce. What compensates for all this loss and makes sowing the seed profitable is that some seed falls on good ground and reproduces itself 30, 60 and 100-fold.

But this is not just true for the farmer; it is true for every person that has ever lived. It is true for the Christian and the non-Christian alike. It is true both negatively and positively. When we sow the wrong, we are going to reap more than we sowed. When we sow the good we likewise will reap a harvest of good.

The Direct Statements of Scripture

This law is emphasized emphatically in two passages. Proverbs 22:8 reads: "He that soweth iniquity shall reap calamity" (literal translation). Unfortunately, even some of the more recent translations translate the word "calamity" אָוֶן as "vanity." However, the word does not refer just to something that is empty or vain; but it has a number of other meanings. It may refer, according to Gesenius, to *falsehood, fraud* (Psalm 36:4; Proverbs 17:4). It may refer to *wickedness, iniquity* (Numbers 23:21; Job 36:21; Isaiah 1:13) and it may refer to *misfortune, adverse circumstances, calamity* (Psalms 55:4; 90:10: Job 15:35; Habakkuk 3:7). In this last sense it signifies also *sorrow* and *grief.* For instance when Rachel was involved in the childbirth in which she died, she called the child's name, Benoni, i.e. "Son of sorrow"—this same word (Genesis 35:18); but Israel named him Benjamin, or "Son of my right hand." The "bread of mourners" (Hosea 9:4) is the same word again; it is the bread of calamity, of adverse circumstance. Thus we can get a feeling for this word and what it signifies. God says that when a person sows "wickedness" he shall reap a harvest of adverse circumstances that involve sorrow, grief, suffering, anxiety, and you have it! Why? Because this is the law of the harvest.

A second passage that establishes this principle is found in Hosea 8:7, "They have sown the wind, and they will reap the whirlwind." The whirlwind is a Hebrew intensive form, "The violent whirlwind." God's message is that you do not just reap in kind—"sow . . . wind . . . reap . . . wind." This is only a part of the whole truth that is involved. Rather the idea paraphrased is "sow . . .wind . . . reap violent, destructive tornado!"

The Principle Illustrated in Jacob

Jacob gives us a vivid example of the law of the harvest. In Genesis 27, Rebekah overheard her husband Isaac telling the oldest of two twin boys to go out and get some venison and prepare a tasty meat dish for him, and then he would give a blessing to him. Rebekah wanted her second born to have that blessing, not Esau, her first born; so she told Jacob to follow her advice implicitly. He was to kill two good kids from among the goats and she would prepare the tasty meat dish for Isaac from this. Since Esau was a hairy man and Jacob was a smooth person, Jacob was to put on the outdoor clothes of his brother. Rebekah then covered his hands and his neck with skins of the kids of the goats. Then he went in to the tent of his father, and the deception worked. He had just gotten the blessing and left, when who should come in, but Esau. The deception didn't last very long; but Isaac had given the blessing to Jacob, and he could not go back on his word.

Rebekah and Jacob had sown seeds in this incident that were to grow and reproduce in like kind—and in more abundance. To exhaust all that is involved here would require a series of messages, but let us see how the law of the harvest comes into play. First of all, Jacob was forced because of what he had done to leave; for Esau threatened that whenever his father passed on, he would kill Jacob. Rebekah did not feel it safe for Jacob to remain at home; so she sent him away to live with her brother Laban in Haran. She said it would just have to be for "a few days, until thy brother's fury turn away" (Genesis 27:44). "Then," she said, "I will send, and fetch thee from thence." Little did Rebekah realize she would never see her son again. She died before he returned, and *she had no one to blame but herself.*

When we follow Jacob, the harvest really becomes evident. Jacob had schemed against his elder brother and by deception obtained the blessing from his father. Now he was to receive in like kind, and even more severely. First, he received Leah as his wife in the place of Rachel whom he loved (Genesis 29). Laban was to teach him something concerning the rights of the firstborn that he would never forget. It is one thing to cheat your brother; it is another thing to be cheated in the wife you receive. But that was just the beginning. The disagreement evident between Isaac and Rebekah over their two boys was sown in their children and it bloomed fully in the problems that existed in Jacob's household. While Jacob and his brother Esau had a few disagreements, it was nothing like the problems between Leah's children, along with the children of her handmaid, and Rachel's children, along with the children of her handmaid. Jacob had sown the wind and he reaped the violent whirlwind. His own sons schemed against him by taking Joseph and selling him into Egypt. Then they took his coat of many colors, killed a kid of the goats and dipped the coat in blood, saying to their father that evidently a wild animal had killed Joseph. For many, many years Jacob was to know nothing different than that Joseph was dead.

He had schemed; he was to reap a far more vicious scheme. He had deceived for a short time; he was to be deceived and to sorrow for an exceedingly long time. A kid of the goats was used by him, and it was to be used against him. He put on clothes and someone was to deceive him with clothes. But Jacob reaped far more in heartache, grief, and suffering, so much so that when Jacob wanted to receive grain from Egypt a second time he said: "Joseph is not, and Simeon is not, and ye will take Benjamin away: all these things are against me" (Genesis 42:36). Later, when Jacob did go down himself to Egypt and he did meet Joseph, he said to Pharaoh: "The days of the years of my pilgrimage are an hundred and thirty years: few and evil have the days of the years of my life been . . . " (Genesis 47:9). Oh how true, how true! Jacob had reaped according to the laws of the harvest.

The Principle Illustrated in David

Perhaps no person in Scripture shows this same principle with any greater clarity than David. So important is this in David's life that the entire book of 2 Samuel is devoted to emphasizing forcibly this one truth. In 2 Samuel everything David does is blessed of God—in the first half of the book. But then David sins with Bathsheba (ch. 11 and 12). From that point on everything falls apart, for David has nothing but trouble. The book moves from triumphs to troubles, from fame to shame, from success to sorrow. First, there was trouble in David's family, and then in his government; first, in his house and then in his kingdom. Here one man sinned and a chain reaction of events was set into motion that was to cause hardship and heartache to untold numbers of individuals and also give occasion for the enemies of God to blaspheme the name of our God. How true it is as Paul said in Romans 14:7, "None of us liveth to himself, and no man dieth to himself." What we do, even in private, may play an important part in the affairs of state and the history of the world. But the worst thing of all is what we do to ourselves and to our families. The higher we are in places of authority, the more careful we must be because what we do affects that many more people.

The events in David's life went like this. At a time when kings go out to battle, David just sent Joab his general, and he remained in Jerusalem. The commander-in-chief was not with his troops although this was where he was supposed to be. His army was involved in a crucial campaign. Being in the wrong place at the wrong time, he did a wrong thing. Walking upon the roof of his palace at evening, he saw a beautiful woman bathing herself. She was so beautiful he sent to inquire who she was. He found out that this was Bathsheba, the wife of one of his soldiers, Uriah, the Hittite. Then he sent for her. This entire episode started out with the incidental and insignificant, but things kept growing with one event piling on another. This is just what sin does. It starts out so insignificantly that it is hardly noticed, but it keeps growing until it has enslaved its captive.

John Wesley's mother wrote to him these significant words: "Whatever weakens your reason, impairs the tenderness of your conscience, obscures your sense of God, or takes off the relish of spiritual things—whatever increases the authority of your body over your mind—that thing to you is sin."

Bathsheba later sent a message back to David that she was with child and that the child was David's. At this point David had an important decision to make, and he made the wrong one. The principle is "he that covereth his sins shall not prosper: but whoso confesseth and forsaketh them shall have mercy" (Proverbs 28:13). Had David judged himself here and stopped his wrong path, things would not have been as terrible as they became, because David went on and on sinning more and more.

He tried to cover his sin first by getting Uriah, Bathsheba's husband, to go home (2 Samuel 11:8). David thought maybe he would think the child was his then, but just born a little prematurely. That didn't work, for, being a good soldier Uriah felt he could not go home while the rest of the army was fighting in battle. So David tried to make him drunk, hoping his convictions would be dulled so he would go home (11:13). When this failed also, David sent word to his general, Joab, to have Uriah placed in the front lines of battle so that he would be killed (11:14-15). Now no one need know that the child was not Uriah's. Uriah was killed in battle, and Bathsheba mourned for her husband. But when the days of mourning were past, David took her into his house and she became his wife. "But the thing that David had done displeased the Lord" (2 Samuel 11:27). Little does man realize the seriousness of sin. Man excuses sin, but God hates it and calls it for what it is.

> Man calls sin an accident; God calls it an abomination.
> Man calls sin a blunder; God calls it blindness.
> Man calls sin a carelessness; God calls it a catastrophe.
> Man calls sin a defect; God calls it a defilement.
> Man calls sin an error; God calls it an estrangement.
> Man calls sin infirmity; God calls it iniquity.

Man calls sin a lapse; God calls it lawlessness.
Man calls sin a mistake; God calls it madness.
Man calls sin reasonable; God calls it rebellion.
Man calls sin a trifle; God calls it a tragedy.
Man calls sin a weakness; God calls it willfulness.

David lived with his sin with Bathsheba and all of its involvements for some time (cf. 2 Samuel 11). God gave David time to judge himself (cf. 1 Corinthians 11:31-32); but since he would not, God sent Nathan the prophet to David. And Nathan had a story to tell to his King.

"There were two men in one city; the one rich, and the other poor. The rich man had exceeding many flocks and herds: but the poor man had nothing, save one little ewe lamb, which he had bought and nourished up: and it grew up together with him, and with his children; it did eat of his own meat, and drank of his own cup, and lay in his bosom, and was unto him as a daughter. And there came a traveller unto the rich man, and he spared to take of his own flock and of his own herd, to dress for the wayfaring man that was come unto him; but took the poor man's lamb, and dressed it for the man that was come to him. And David's anger was greatly kindled against the man; and he said to Nathan, As the Lord liveth, the man that hath done this thing shall surely die [or, 'deserves to die'] : and he shall restore the lamb fourfold, because he did this thing, and because he had no pity" (2 Samuel 12:1-6). It is a characteristic trait seen in the Word where the Lord lets us pronounce our own judgment (cf. Job 9:20; Psalm 64:1-8; Luke 19:22).

All that was left for Nathan to give was the punch line and pronounce the judgment. So as God's spokesman Nathan fearlessly said to David, "Thou art the man" (12:7).

Right at this point David's entire character is brought to light. He did not try to excuse his sin or add to his sin by having Nathan killed, which he could have done. Rather he repented immediately, and Psalm 51 gives to us his prayer of repentance. David had been miserable in his sin and was only too glad to be restored back into fellowship with the Lord. It was this attitude that made David "a man after God's own heart." Beloved, there is a vast difference between being sorry for sin and being sorry you were caught, between confessing your sins and confessing someone else's involvement, between seeing your own faults and seeing some other person's. All too many times we join with Adam and say as he did when God questioned him about his wrong doing, "Lord, it is because of the wife *You* gave me." This, supposedly, got Adam off the hook.

A little girl took scissors and cut large chunks out of her long hair. Sometime later, she walked into the room where her mother was. The mother said in anquish, "O baby! you have cut your hair!"

The child gaped in astonishment and said, "But how did you know, mummy? I hid it very carefully in the wastebasket."

Many are just as foolish about their sins as this little girl was about her hair. We all need to be reminded that "all things are naked and opened unto the eyes of him with whom we have to do" (Hebrews 4:13).

Nathan went on to make three charges against David, stating emphatically the sin David had done and then pronouncing the judgment that David would reap because of his sin. They are as follows:

1. You killed Uriah (2 Samuel 12:9).
    The judgment: The sword will never depart from your house (12:10).
2. You took his wife (12:9).
    The judgment: Your wives will be taken before your eyes (12:11).
3. You did this secretly (12:12).
    The judgment: Your wives will be defiled openly before all Israel (12:11-12).

This is the law of the harvest, and we need to understand it because no one is going to get around this law. The judgment is always greater than the sin because you always reap more than you sow. David had pronounced: "The man that hath done this thing . . . shall restore the lamb fourfold, because he did this thing, and because he had no pity" (2 Samuel 12:5-6). This was exactly the penalty prescribed in the law. According to Exodus 22:4 if someone stole an "ox, or ass, or sheep," and the animal was found alive in his hand, then he was to restore double. However in Exodus 22:1 the law required that whenever a man had killed a sheep, he was to restore fourfold. David had killed a man, and he was to pay fourfold, and he did. Four of David's sons died premature deaths (Shimea, 2 Samuel 12:19; Amnon, 2 Samuel 13:28-29; Absalom, 2 Samuel 18:14; Adonijah, 1 Kings 2:24-25). This is the law of the harvest. It is law and not grace. It shows no mercy because it is a fixed and irrevocable law that no one can get around. The sooner one stops sowing to the flesh, the sooner he will stop reaping in like kind. The sooner one starts sowing the good, the sooner he will begin reaping the same.

Again, let it be repeated that this is why Paul so forcibly stresses in Galatians 6 that even during this present age of grace we are not to be deceived, thinking we can sow to the flesh and not reap the full consequences of our actions. And the full consequences are that we always reap more than we sow. This fact was emphasized vividly to Israel under the law as seen in the five cycles of discipline (Leviticus 26:14-46). Whenever Israel followed the Lord and obeyed His laws, they would be blessed abundantly (26:3-13). But whenever they disobeyed the Lord, the consequence was that they would experience terror, consumption and burning fever that would sap their strength and life. Even though they sowed their seed, their enemies would eat their harvest. They would fail in battle, and become servants to their enemies. They would be so jittery that they would take flight when no one was pursuing (26:16-17). This is what they were to reap because they had sown the wrong in disobeying the commandments of the Lord.

But as we find out, that was just the beginning. For these things were sent upon them to cause them to harken—to wake them up; but if it did not do it, then they were sowing even more iniquity and would reap accordingly. In the words of the Lord: "And if ye will not yet for all this harken unto me, then I will punish you seven times more for your sins" (26:18). The former unit of discipline is now increased sevenfold, and God again states what He would do (26:19-20). If that does not work, another increase will be felt by the Nation, seven times greater than what previously came (26:21). This, beloved, is not addition; it is multiplication! What began as one unit of discipline has now become, under the third cycle, forty-nine units.

But again this is not the end. There are two more increases, each seven times the previous one so that the fifth cycle of discipline is 2401 units of discipline (1 x 7 x 7 x 7 x 7). This is the law of sowing and reaping; for, under each cycle, they were sowing the sin which reaped the greater discipline. While we are not under the Mosaic law today, the eternal principles of the moral law of God abide for all time to all people.

The Positive Aspects

Now it would be amiss if it were left there with just the negative, for the principle does not only work in judgment and discipline, but equally in blessing. For example, God's only criticism of David was this incident with Bathsheba as is seen by the record of the prophet in 1 Kings 15:5, "David did that which was right in the eyes of the Lord and turned not aside from any thing that he commanded him all the days of his life, save only in the matter of Uriah the Hittite." Therefore, most of David's life was sowing the good, not evil; and, as a result, God continued to bless many of the kings of Judah for many years for David's sake because he had done that which was right (cf. 1 Kings 11:12; 15:4; 2 Kings 8:19; 14:3; 16:2; 18:3; 19:34; 20:6; 22:2). Blessings from this righteous man's life were to be reaped for many years after he was gone because he had sown a bountiful harvest of good. He was the standard of righteousness, according to Scripture, for all the kings who followed, for each king's life was compared to that of King David.

But what about us today? In Philippians 4:6 and 7 we read: "Be careful [anxious] for nothing; but in every thing by prayer and supplication with thanksgiving let your requests be made known unto God. And the peace of God, which passeth all understanding, shall keep your hearts and minds through Christ Jesus." Just as the unbeliever and carnal Christian who sows sin cycles in calamities of all the varieties with their accompanying anxieties (cf. Leviticus 26:36), the believer living in fellowship with the Lord will cycle in peace. Paul shows in these verses that when we relate to the Lord, "the God of peace," a guard is placed around both our hearts and minds—the emotions and the intellect—so that we are protected all the more from further attack. Thus we go from peace to more peace, while the path of sin moves in the opposite way from anxiety to more anxiety. You just cannot lose when walking in fellowship with the Lord, and you cannot gain when walking out of fellowship with Him. Therefore, as we have opportunity, let us do good unto all men, especially unto them who are of the household of faith (Galatians 6:10).

5

DOING

Perhaps you heard about the man who was in the hospital suffering from a bad heart attack when his family received word that he had fallen heir to a million dollars. Fearing that the news might be too much of a shock to the man, they asked his pastor to give him the information very gently. The pastor decided to approach him like this: "What would you do if you inherited the sum of a million dollars?" "Why," he replied, "I'd give half of it to the church." The pastor dropped dead!

The laws of the harvest contain another very significant truth.

LAW #5.   WE REAP IN PROPORTION AS WE SOW.

If one does not sow, he does not reap. If he sows sparingly, he reaps sparingly. If he wants to reap a bountiful harvest, he must sow in a bountiful way. If the farmer only cultivates one acre, he can only reap what one acre can produce. However, if he has one hundred acres under cultivation, his harvest can be one hundred times greater.

A difference needs to be observed between this principle and the previous one which stated that we always reap more than we sow. Both are true at the same time; yet this principle that we reap in proportion as we sow in no way affects the fact that we also reap more than we sow. Both laws have to do with quantity or amount. However, the previous law was God's part, and this law has to do with our part. God's part is that whatever seed is sown is multiplied many fold. Our part is that we need to sow all the good that we can. "Cast thy bread upon the waters: for thou shalt find it after many days. Give a portion to seven, and also to eight; for thou knowest not what evil shall be upon the earth . . . In the morning sow thy seed, and in the evening withhold not thine hand: for thou knowest not whether shall prosper, either this or that, or whether they both shall be alike good" (Ecclesiastes 11:1, 2, 6).

The Principle Stated

Paul states this law clearly as he devotes two whole chapters in his Second letter to the Corinthians to the subject of giving. His statement is, "He which soweth sparingly shall reap also sparingly; and he which soweth bountifully shall reap also bountifully" (2 Corinthians 9:6). This is the way things are, and there is no getting around it.

> "If you want to be rich . . . GIVE!
> If you want to be poor . . . GRASP!
> If you want abundance . . . SCATTER!
> If you want to be needy . . . HOARD!"

This law operates both negatively and positively. The more one sows to the flesh, the more he will reap the corruption which the flesh alone can produce. But equally true, the more one sows to the Spirit, the more he reaps the blessings of a righteous harvest. "The fruit of righteousness is sown in peace of them that make peace" (James 3:18). This principle can be illustrated again by the life of David. Had David merely sinned in the episode with Bathsheba, his sin would be grave enough. But since he never stopped sowing to the flesh but went on and on until he had killed Bathsheba's husband, he was to reap all the more from his actions because he had sown all the more wickedness.

Now it may be said for all of us: "There is not a just man upon the earth, that doeth good, and sinneth not" (Ecclesiastes 7:20). But as Christians and believers, we who know the Lord need to stop the moment we have sinned and confess our sin. The moment we do this, we stop the process of sowing to the flesh. Then God is able to be faithful toward us and righteous toward Himself on the basis of the cross work of Christ and forgive us our sin and cleanse us from all unrighteousnes (1 John 1:9). However, it is always better to practice preventive medicine than emergency surgery, and, therefore, we need to learn to walk in the Spirit; and, when we do, we will not fulfill the lusts of the flesh (Galatians 5:16). It is possible to learn so to walk, else the command is without significance. Walking in the Spirit produces in our lives the fruit of the Spirit and gives us nothing of which we may be ashamed.

Positive Sowing

Stating the principle positively, as believers we are to be "zealous of good works" (Titus 2:14), "ready to every good work" (Titus 3:1), and "careful to maintain good works" (Titus 3:8). When the young lad gave his five loaves and two fish to the Lord Jesus Christ, the Lord took and multiplied them to feed five thousand men besides women and children. This gives us some example of the law of the harvest. The "Sunday School Times" says Captain Levy of Philadelphia, when asked how he was able to give so much to the Lord's work and still have so much left, answered, "Oh, as I shovel out, He shovels in; and the Lord has a bigger shovel than I do."

Our Lord Himself said, as is recorded for us in the Book of Acts, "It is more blessed to give than to receive" (Acts 20:35). Moreover, His whole life and His death were a living demonstration of this fact. His words to those who would be His disciples were: "Give, and it shall be given unto you; good measure, pressed down, and shaken together, and running over, shall men give into your bosom. For with the same measure that ye mete withal it shall be measured to you again" (Luke 6:38).

This same truth is stressed in the Old Testament as well. "The liberal soul shall be made fat: and he that watereth shall be watered also himself" (Proverbs 11:25). "He that hath pity upon the poor lendeth unto the Lord; and that which he hath given will he pay him again" (Proverbs 19:17). However, we need to realize that God's method of repayment is not like man's. He does not give back merely what we have given, but He returns with interest. Now His interest is not a meager six per cent or even a colossal twelve per cent. Listen to this percentage paid by the Lord found in Matthew 19:29. "And every one that hath forsaken houses, or brethren, or sisters, or father, or mother, or wife, or children, or lands, for my name's sake, shall receive an hundredfold, and shall inherit everlasting life." Receiving an hundredfold is a 10,000 per cent dividend returned on one's investment. This is what kind of repayment God gives.

Furthermore in Proverbs we read: "He that giveth unto the poor shall not lack" (Proverbs 28:27). The Lord will see to it that every need is supplied. However, the verse goes on to read: "but he that hideth his eyes shall have many a curse." So great is this truth that the entire 58th chapter of Isaiah is devoted to it. The people were keeping a fast day as a legalistic ritual of worship, and God was not accepting it (v. 5). However, the Lord talks about the fast He does accept: "Is not this the fast that I have chosen? to loose the bands of wickedness, to undo heavy burdens, and to let the oppressed go free, and that ye break every yoke? Is it not to deal thy bread to the hungry, and that thou bring the poor that are cast out to thy house? when thou seeth the naked, that thou cover him; and that thou hide not thyself from thine own flesh?" (vv. 6-7). Then the Lord speaks about what He will do; and what He does in blessing is far more than what they did (vv. 8-14). In other words,

God will repay them in accordance with the laws of the harvest. They sowed, and they will receive bountifully from Him above and beyond their hopes and expectations.

In the New Testament we find the same emphasis. Ephesians 3:20 says: "Now unto him that is able to do exceeding abundantly above all that we ask or think . . . " Notice carefully, that our God wants to do for us (1) "what we ask" and even what we "think." But He wants and is able to do (2) "all that we ask or think." Yet He is such a great God that He wants to bless us (3) "above all that we ask or think." But still we should never limit His blessings to this, for it is His desire to bless us (4) "abundantly above all that we ask or think." However, this is even yet not the extent of His blessings to us; for He purposes in accordance with the laws of the harvest to bless us (5) "exceeding abundantly above all that we ask or think." All we have to do is meet the condition for blessing.

The Condition for Blessing

What is this condition? Whether we want to face the issue or not, it has to do with our relationship to material possessions. Every offering that is spoken of in the New Testament is an offering for the poor or for those in need. While the Bible refers to prayer about 500 times, to faith less than 500 times, it refers to material possessions about 1,000 times. Nearly one-half of the parables of our Lord have to do with stewardship of material possessions. Why is this so? Because money and possessions affect us greatly whether we want to admit it or not.

It is possible to cross over a very fine line so that no longer do we possess things, but things possess us. How much will it take to satisfy a greedy person? He is never satisfied; for, when he has $100,000, he wants $200,000, then half a million; but still he is not satisfied. Neither does one million or 10 million satisfy. "He that loveth silver shall not be satisfied with silver; nor he that loveth abundance with increase" (Ecclesiastes 5:10). The cravings of man are never satisfied by the empty things of this life.

Luther says: "An exemplification of this may be found in that renowned king and praiseworthy hero, Alexander the Great. In a very brief space of time (for in all he did not reign more than twelve years) he subjugated to himself a large portion of the whole world: and notwithstanding, once upon a time, when he heard a philosopher arguing that there are more worlds than one, he sighed deeply, and said, 'Alas! that I have not as yet subdued more than one world!' So, if he had at once gained ten other worlds, his heart would not have found rest: nay more, it would not have been satisfied with a thousand, or even with countless worlds."

> "The folks who spend their days
> In buying cars and clothes and rings
> Don't seem to know that empty lives
> Are just as empty filled with things!"

Stewards for God

But the problem for the believer is that "covetousness . . . is idolatry" (Colossians 3:5), and the "covetous man . . . is an idolater" (Ephesians 5:5). Thus while we might never bow before idols of wood and stone, yet there are the idols of the heart that are just as real and just as destructive to the spiritual life. For this reason the Lord admonishes His disciples: "Lay not up for yourselves treasures upon earth, where moth and rust doth corrupt, and where thieves break through and steal: but lay up for yourselves treasures in heaven, where neither moth nor rust doth corrupt, and where thieves do not break through nor steal: for where your treasure is, there will your heart be also" (Matthew 6:19-21). The last statement here is the key to it all. Only as we are making heaven the place of our reward are we going to use money and material possessions wisely in light of eternity. This is exactly what our Lord instructs us to do in the parable of Luke 16. We are to so live our lives down here on earth that we use the mammon of unrighteousness, or money, to the advantage of God's glory. We are to spend and invest it in light of eternity when we no longer have any stewardship responsibility (vv. 1-9).

When your stewardship and mine are examined by the Lord Jesus Christ will He be able to commend us or not? Will He be able to say we were wise in our use of money and have invested it in light of eternity or will He say we missed our opportunity completely? In Luke 16:13 the Lord clearly says: "No servant can serve two masters . . . Ye cannot serve God and mammon."

Be honest! Who really controls your life and your giving? Billy Sunday used to say a man had two conversions. One was of his soul and the other was of his pocketbook. Dr. R. E. Neighbor tells the account that when he was in the baptistry with a railway engineer ready to proceed with the baptismal service, his candidate whispered: "Wait! I forgot something. I want to return to the robing room, and get my pocketbook and let you baptize it with me!" Oh, would that all of us gave God our pocketbook, for God says, "Them that honor me I will honor." (1 Samuel 2:30). Besides, it is the Lord that enables all of us to work and gain wealth (Deuteronomy 8:18).

Paul instructs Timothy: "Charge them that are rich in this world, that they be not highminded, nor trust in uncertain riches, but in the living God, who giveth us richly all things to enjoy; that they do good, that they be rich in good works, ready to distribute, willing to communicate; laying up in store for themselves a good foundation against the time to come . . . " (1 Timothy 6:17-19). The excellent thing to do is, "Do your givin' while you're livin' so you're knowin' where it's goin'."

When a rich man died it was asked: "How much did he leave?" The reply came: "He left it all!" The problem as it turns out to be so often is that it is left for children to fight over and for Uncle Sam and the lawyers to acquire.

That is not being good stewards for God. "For we brought nothing into this world, and it is certain we can carry nothing out" (1 Timothy 6:7).

The late R. G. LeTourneau wrote: "I kept saying to myself, 'Next year I will have a lot of money for the Lord. I will be true to Him later.' I did not know that NOW is the Lord's time. So the question is not, 'How much of my money do I give to God' but 'How much of His money do I keep for myself?' "

> "It's not what I'd do with a million,
> If riches e'er fell to my lot,
> But it's what I will do at the present
> With the ten dollar bill that I've got."

It has been said there are three kinds of givers—the flint, the sponge and the honeycomb. To get anything out of the flint, you must hammer it, and then you get only chips and sparks. To get water out of a sponge, you must squeeze it, and the more you squeeze, the more you get. But the honeycomb just overflows with its own sweetness. Some people are stingy and hard; they give nothing away if they can help it. Others are goodnatured; they yield to pressure; and the more they are pressed the more they will give. A few delight in giving without being asked at all; and of these the Bible says, "The Lord loveth a cheerful giver."

Recipients and Custodians

There is not a thing that we can give to God that He has not first given to us.

We only are recipients and custodians, but the Father seems to want us to manifest how much we trust Him and how truly grateful we are for His blessings. Having received from His hand freely and bountifully, how will we give? The cup He presents us is always running over. He does not give just a calf; it is the fatted calf. The robe He puts on us is the best robe. The joy is unspeakable and full of glory; the peace is that which passeth understanding: the love passeth knowledge; His grace superabounds. Now all the Father wants from us is a heart that overflows in gratitude and does for others as it has received itself. Someone has well said: "Giving is not just a way of raising money; it is a way of raising men."

"Nuggets of Truth" contained an announcement that a new collection plate had been invented with some very unique features. When you drop in a quarter or more, it doesn't make a sound; you drop in a dime and it tinkles like a bell; a nickel blows like a whistle; and a penny fires a shot; when you don't drop in anything, it takes your picture. The truth of the matter is that the Lord stands over against the treasury and knows exactly how much each of us gives.

> Five thousand for my convertible,
> Ten thousand for a piece of sod,
> Twenty thousand I paid to be in a house,
> A dollar I gave to God.
> A sum to entertain
> My friends in endless chatter;
> And when the world goes crazy mad,
> I ask: "Lord, what's the matter?"
> Yet there is one big question—
> And for its answer I now search—
> With things so bad in this old world,
> What's holding back my church?

The Christian's Example and Paradox

We all need the admonition Paul gave to the Philippians: "Look not every man on his own things, but every man also on the things of others. Let this mind be in you, which was also in Christ Jesus" (Philippians 2:4-5). He never thought of Himself but thought only of others. If there were ever an example of the positive aspect of the laws of the harvest, it is seen in the life of the Lord Jesus Christ. He gave Himself for us. Each of us in turn determines the kind of harvest we will have and also the amount. We determine both its quality and its quantity.

C. H. Spurgeon said a number of years ago concerning the paradoxes of the Christian life: "To get, we must give; to accumulate, we must scatter; to make ourselves happy, we must make others happy; and in order to become spiritually vigorous, we must seek the spiritual good of others." All of us need to increase both the quality and the quantity of our lives in light of eternity. Every one of us needs to live up to our full potential.

When Charles H. Spurgeon wrote, he used the pen name of John Ploughman. I want to conclude this study with a shortened version of his work entitled, *Scatter and Increase* which emphasized this truth vividly.

"People will not believe it, and yet it is true as the gospel, that giving leads to thriving. John Bunyan said,

> There was a man, and some did count him mad,
> The more he gave away, the more he had.

He had an old saying to back him, one which is as old as the hills, as good as gold—

> Give and spend
> And God will send.

"If a man cannot pay his debts he must not think of giving, for he has nothing of his own, and it is stealing to give away other people's property. Be just before you are generous. Don't give to Peter what is due to Paul. They used to say that 'Give' is dead, and 'Restore' is buried, but I do not believe it any more than I do another saying, 'There are only two good men, one is dead, and the other is not born.' No, no: there are still many free hearts, and John Ploughman knows quite a few of them—people who don't cry, 'Go next door,' but who say, 'Here's a little help, and we wish we could make it ten times as much!

God has often a great share in a small house, and many a little man has a large heart.

"Now, you will find that generous people are happy people, and get more enjoyment out of what they have than miserly folks. Misers never rest till they are dead: they often get so wretched that they would hang themselves only they grudge the expense of a rope. Generous souls are happy by the happiness of others. The money they give to the poor buys them more pleasure than any other that they spend.

"I have seen men of means give pennies, and they have been cheap in everything. They carried on a tin-pot business, lived like beggars, and died like dogs. I have seen others give to the poor and to the cause of God by shovelfuls and they have wheelbarrow loads. They made good use of their stewardship, and the great Lord has trusted them with more, while the bells in their hearts have rung out merry peals when they have thought of widows who blessed them, and orphan children who smiled into their faces. Let us see what we can do to scatter joy all around us, just as the sun throws its light on hill and dale.

"He that gives God his heart will not deny him his money. He will take a pleasure in giving, but he will not wish to be seen, nor will he expect to have a dollar's worth of humor for a nickel. He will look out for worthy objects; for giving to lazy, spendthrifts is wasteful and wicked; you might as well sugar a brick and think to turn it into a pudding. A wise man will go to work in a sensible way, and will give his money to worthy persons as to the Lord. No security can be better and no interest can be surer. The Bank is open at all hours. It is the best Savings' Bank in the nation."

6

PERSEVERING

LAW #6   WE REAP THE FULL HARVEST OF THE
GOOD ONLY IF WE PERSEVERE; THE EVIL
COMES TO HARVEST ON ITS OWN.

The problem of the average believer today is not a lack of knowledge, but the application of truths he already knows. He is carrying around many facts he has never integrated into life. Along a Kentucky highway was parked a mammoth motor truck van. The driver was standing by the tractor from which a front wheel had been removed. A preacher stopped to see if he needed any assistance, but the trucker thanked him and said he had already sent for help. He had burned out a wheel bearing, and another one was on its way. As the preacher pulled away, his eyes caught the lettering on the side of the van: *Standard Oil Company of Kentucky, Lubricants Division.* He had burned out a bearing—hauling grease. Many a Christian has failed in his own life while seeking to minister to others. We do not dare let weeds grow in our own garden while we hoe them out of others. The farmer who labors must be first partaker of the fruits of his own garden (2 Timothy 2:6). This is not selfishness; it is survival.

This brings forth another aspect of the harvest. Paul's admonition in Galatians 6:9 was, "And let us not be weary in well doing: for in due season we shall reap, if we faint not." Thus another principle is stated here which every gardener knows.

LAW #6. WE REAP THE FULL HARVEST OF THE GOOD ONLY IF WE PERSEVERE; THE EVIL COMES TO HARVEST ON ITS OWN.

Everyone who tills the ground knows that a vegetable garden cannot be planted and then forgotten. If it is, very little will come from the planting. What a garden requires is much labor and work in order to reap an abundant harvest. But in God's program of things, this is not true of the weeds. When the thorn and briar seeds are sown, they have the ability to come to a harvest on their own without anyone doing a thing.

The Spiritual Aspects

Now, what is true in the natural realm is true also in the spiritual realm. The only way we will enjoy the blessings of a full harvest of the good things sown is to persevere and not faint. Once the evil is sown, however, it comes to fruition on its own; but the good will never produce an abundant harvest without constant attention. What this is saying, then, is that there are going to be problems and difficulties; and we can expect them and depend upon them. Even though we sow to the Spirit (Galatians 6:8), this does not mean that there will not be opposition. Somehow we have the feeling that if we do things right, there should be no problems. This is not so. Even the Son of man who sowed the good seed had an enemy come along behind and sow tares (Matthew 13:24-30; 36-43). If this happened for Him, how can we expect less. Whenever the saints say, "Let's rise up and build," the enemy will be right behind to rise up and oppose. Whenever there is a great door and effectual opened to us, there will right along with it be many adversaries (1 Corinthians 16:9).

Through these problems and difficulties God is seeking to work virtues into our lives: trust in Him, that He will bring things to completion; patience in the time of difficulties, that we do not lose heart; perseverance in the work, knowing that our labor is not in vain in the Lord; and discipline, so that we do not allow difficulties to overwhelm us and defeat us. Each Christian on the pilgrimage of faith is forced to work through the very same problems that faced all those who went before him.

"Wherefore seeing we also are compassed about with so great a cloud of witnesses, let us lay aside every weight, and the sin which doth so easily beset us, and let us run with patience the race that is set before us, looking unto Jesus the author and finisher of our faith; who for the joy that was set before him endured the cross, despising the shame, and is set down at the right hand of the throne of God. For consider him that endured such contradiction of sinners against himself, lest ye be wearied and faint in your minds" (Hebrews 12:1-3). Realizing this, let us look at some of the ingredients God is using to force us to grow and mature.

An Example in the Life of Paul

God's design in allowing difficulties is not that they should defeat us, but that they make us exactly what He wants us to be. When Paul was faced with opposition and persecution, he could say: "None of these things move me" (Acts 20:24), but he made this statement after he had walked with the Lord for a number of years. At this point in Paul's life, he had been laboring for the Savior for 20 years. He was burdened to go to Jerusalem and there to suffer and even die, if need be. While he was there, he was taken into custody and ultimately kept in prison in Caesarea for two years. At the very beginning of his imprisonment, the Lord revealed to him that he would ultimately go to Rome (Acts 23:11); but why the delay and the time in confinement? Even after Paul arrived in Rome, he was still to spend two more years under house arrest and then a time of confinement again after which he was released.

Now God makes no mistakes with any of us, and neither was He making a mistake with His apostle who was so active and zealous for Him. The Lord was graciously working in Paul's life to take him aside from the vigorous activities in which he was engaged and force him to have time alone to meditate and reflect—time which, undoubtedly, otherwise he would not have taken. Meditation is what produces depth, and this depth of reflection was to be manifested in the epistles that were to come from Paul ultimately in his Roman imprisonment. It was during this time that he wrote the epistles of Ephesians, Philippians, Colossians and Philemon. In these epistles there is nothing that would in any way contradict what he previously had written in his earlier epistles of 1 and 2 Thessalonians, Galatians, Romans, and 1 and 2 Corinthians; but there is a vast difference in his former and latter epistles in the very breadth, height and depth of the subjects covered. In all the epistles, the Christ Paul met on the Damascus road is central; but in the prison epistles He is the exalted and glorified One. It is the emphasis that is different. An analysis of this difference is as follows:

Earlier Epistles	*Prison Epistles*
The visible realm	The invisible realm
Both unbelievers and believers	Almost completely with believers
The historical realm (of spiritual truths)	The spiritual realm (of historical truths)
Deals with facts	Deals with the significance of facts
Our union with Christ	Our communion with Christ
Christ crucified	Christ risen, ascended and exalted
The work of Christ	The person of Christ
Points to the cross	Points from the cross
The milk of the Christian life	The meat of the Christian life
The commencement of the pilgrim life	The advancement of the pilgrim life
Deals with the formation of the church	Deals with the glory and high calling of the church

Neither the person nor work of Christ changed, but Paul changed in his understanding of what the person and work of Christ had accomplished for us.

Paul had learned in his life that whatever came to the believer was from the Lord, and came through the Lord, so that he could glory "in tribulations also: knowing that tribulation worketh patience; and patience, experience; and experience, hope" (Romans 5:3-4). This servant of the Lord knew that all things work together for good to every believer so that he is not to be thrown by pressures and problems since nothing can separate any believer from the love of Christ or the love of the Father (Romans 8:28, 35, 39).

In all that might come upon the child of God, Paul says, "we are more than conquerors through him that loved us" (Romans 8:37). Being more than conquerors, we have not even begun to be tested as to the limits of our strength and endurance under pressure. We could have taken more had it been put upon us. Someone said it well when he wrote: "Never let a difficulty stop you. It may be only sand on the track to keep you from slipping."

> "If your way is dark and gloomy
> And your future black as night,
> Wait; it may be a tunnel
> That's a short-cut to the light."

God's Schooling

If we could see things from God's viewpoint, we could see that the delays of God are only disciplines to prepare us for better things. Before Moses was ready to lead the children of Israel, he needed not only all the education Egypt could provide for him, but he needed to lead sheep on the back side of the desert as well. God was in the one as much as the other. Before David was ever prepared for the throne, he had to learn the patience of waiting on God and trusting Him to bring it to pass. So the Lord allowed

David for a while to be in the court of Saul in order to gain firsthand experience. But then when Saul's attitude changed toward David, he was forced to flee from Saul and trust God in total dependence for everything.

It was during this time he learned not only to know God, but to know people and deal with their problems; for the Scripture says: "And every one that was in distress, and every one that was in debt, and every one that was discontented, gathered themselves unto him; and he became a captain over them" (1 Samuel 22:2). By moving across the land, he learned firsthand about the nation he was later to rule. Whom God uses, he prepares; and there are no exceptions.

An Example in the Life of David

Notice how God was preparing David by the experience that is recorded for us in 1 Samuel 30. "And it came to pass, when David and his men were come to Ziklag on the third day, that the Amalekites had invaded the south, and Ziklag, and smitten Ziklag, and burned it with fire; and had taken the women captives, that were therein: they slew not any, either great or small, but carried them away, and went on their way. So David and his men came to the city, and, behold, it was burned with fire; and their wives, and their sons, and their daughters, were taken captives. Then David and the people that were with him lifted up their voice and wept, until they had no more power to weep. . . . And David was greatly distressed; for the people spake of stoning him, because the soul of all the people was grieved, every man for his sons and for his daughters: but David encouraged himself in the Lord his God" (vv. 1-4, 6).

What is a person to do in a time when everything goes wrong? Here we see the answer. "He encouraged himself in the Lord his God." He did not try to think positively, as good to do as that might be. He did not try to deny reality and say, "You win some and lose some." The people were ready to stone him, and there was no human support. David was cast upon his face before God, and that is just what the Lord wanted. He could not look to man, so he looked to God, his God, the LORD. The word Lord comes from the Hebrew word meaning "I AM." The Lord is the One who IS. He is the living God. He is unchangeable. He is also God, signifying the Mighty One. After encouraging himself in the Lord his God, David, following the Lord's directions, went out and recaptured the people and their possessions without any loss of life.

Waiting on the Lord

Oh, that we might think upon His name (cf. Malachi 3:16) and be encouraged. "Rest in the Lord, and wait patiently for him: fret not thyself because of him who prospereth in his way, because of the man who bringeth wicked devices to pass" (Psalm 37:7). "I waited patiently for the Lord; and he inclined unto me, and heard my cry" (Psalm 40:1). There are times when the most important thing we can do is do nothing. It is that aspect of patience which is to wait until God's time and then move only in accordance with His specific command. Moses learned this (Exodus 14:13-14), Jehoshaphat did (2 Chronicles 20:1-30), and so must we. Yet it is one of the hardest lessons to learn because the flesh wants to *do* rather than *wait* upon God. It is this aspect of waiting that is brought out in Psalm 62:5, "My soul, wait thou only upon God; for my expectation is from him."

Isaiah says: "He giveth power to the faint; and to them that have no might he increaseth strength. Even the youths shall faint and be weary, and the young men shall utterly fall: but they that wait upon the Lord shall renew their strength; they shall mount up with wings as eagles; they shall run, and not be weary; and they shall walk, and not faint" (Isaiah 40:29-31).

If you have no strength, then you are not waiting upon the Lord and thinking upon who He is. By waiting upon Him, you shall have spiritual, moral, and emotional strength—which the passage is speaking about. Waiting upon the Lord will do three things for you: First, you will mount up with wings like eagles. This refers to experiences that are far above anything earthly; you may call them mountain top experiences or whatever you like. The person who waits upon his God shall enjoy such occasions, and he will not often speak about them because they are precious experiences between him and his God. These experiences always result from waiting upon God as He is seen in His Word. This is not something other than Word-oriented.

Secondly, you shall run and not be weary. A time of running involves a stress or crisis. These come suddenly and unexpectedly upon God's children. At such a time, we have the strength to run and not be weary because God has given that strength to us ahead of time and so equipped us for this emergency.

Last of all, you shall walk and not faint. Here are involved the ordinary daily activities of life; and, in them all, He gives us strength so that we do not get weary and faint in the midst of our activities. The reason is because everything is related to Him, and He is then working in and through us. When He is working, we do not grow weary. Hudson Taylor said: "I used to ask God if He would come and help me; then I asked God if I might come and help Him; then I ended by asking God to do His work through me."

Constructive Use of Blunders

Another important area of perseverance is not just adjusting to things that come upon us over which we have no control, but handling mistakes that we have made because of our own blundering. None of us is without them; and, therefore, greatness does not consist in not making mistakes, but in what we do with them. If we can use them constructively and learn from them so as not to repeat a failure, then we are wise indeed. If we allow them to overwhelm and defeat us so that we no longer even try to succeed, then we shall neither persevere nor reap the harvest of blessing God has intended for our lives.

No one can sit down at a typewriter for the first time

and type away without making mistakes. It takes many hours of patient practice, seeking to press the right keys at the right time with some measure of both speed and accuracy, to be a typist. But even the best typists make mistakes. If you let mistakes defeat you, you are a slave to something rather than its master. This leads to depression and despair. If you hoe up a cabbage by mistake in a garden, this is no reason to hoe up the entire row or the whole garden. If you have taken a wrong road, learn from the experience, because sometime in your life your knowledge will save both you and others a far greater mistake and blunder.

Discouragement

There is no experience through which the child of God goes that the Lord does not want to use positively for blessing. This is why we are to count it all joy when we fall into various testings (James 1:2) which God has designed to mature us (1:3-4) and never to defeat us (1 Corinthians 10:13). It is Satan's work to try to defeat and discourage us. Since Satan cannot keep us from Christ, his next best thing is to keep us from living victoriously in Christ.

"The Gospel Herald" carried this parable that illustrates the point.

"It was advertised that the devil was going to put his tools up for sale. On the date of sale the tools were placed for public inspection, each being marked with its sale price. There were a treacherous lot of implements. Hatred, Envy, Jealousy, Deceit, Lying, Pride, and so on, comprised the outfit. Laid apart from the rest was a harmless-looking tool, well-worn, and priced very high.

" 'What is the name of this tool?' asked one of the purchasers, pointing to it.

" 'That is Discouragement,' the devil replied tersely.

" 'Why have you priced it so high?'

" 'Because it is more useful to me than the others. I can pry open and get inside a man's heart with that, when I cannot get near him with the other tools. Once I get inside, I can make him do what I choose. It is badly worn, because I use it on almost everyone since few people know it belongs to me.'

"The devil's price for Discouragement was so high that it was never sold. Discouragement is still the devil's tool, and he is using it today on God's own people."

There is not a person living who does not at times become discouraged. Paul was so discouraged on one occasion that even he despaired of life itself, as he writes to the Corinthians, "For we would not, brethren, have you ignorant of our trouble which came to us in Asia, that we were pressed out of measure, above strength, insomuch that we despaired even of life" (2 Corinthians 1:8). Since this may happen to all of us, we are exhorted to encourage one another daily (Hebrews 3:13), lest any of us be hardened through the deceitfulness of sin. We are to provoke one another "unto love and good works" (Hebrews 10:24). This word "provoke" tells us to incite, stimulate and spur one another on in a positive way rather than to provoke to wrath and anger. F. B. Meyer is quoted in "Moody Monthly" as saying if he had his preaching ministry to live over again, he would preach more sermons of encouragement to God's people.

The Place and Way to Victory

There is a sense in which we must begin right where we are if we are going to overcome discouragement and find victory. David refreshed himself right where he was in the Lord. The tendency is to try to flee and go somewhere else and have a fresh start, but this is not the Lord's way. When the disciples had toiled all night and caught nothing, the Lord had them fish right where their boat was in the same old place where they had toiled and caught nothing. Why? Because the victory had to be given *there* in the problem or there would have been no victory at all over the discouragement. They would have thought the answer to their problem was to move, rather than to relate to the Lord. Some of us are always running to something else, not realizing that right where we are is where the Lord wants to begin to work.

While we cannot do everything, there is always something we can do in obedience to His command. When He speaks to us in clear voice, "Cast the net on the right side," and we obey, the experience will lead us to further knowledge of His will. The point is this: There is something *we can do*. We are to do it and keep moving on. The Lord at times illuminates before us the whole pathway that we are to take, but at other times it seems we walk as in darkness. No child of God is ever left without light to take one step. "Thy word is a lamp unto my feet, and a light unto my path" (Psalm 119:105). When walking in the darkness, we must obediently take that one step we know to take. Only then will we see clearly to take the next step. We are to keep walking until the light gives out—which, thank God, it never will. The believer that will not be obedient to take the step he sees will never have any additional light or guidance.

The highest mountain can be conquered, but the top can be reached only one step at a time. The greatest task can be achieved if we will but take it little by little. During the time of Nehemiah when the wall was being rebuilt, the people complained, "The strength of the bearers of burdens is decayed, and there is much rubbish; so that we are not able to build the wall" (Nehemiah 4:10). Discouragement had set in because of all the rubbish and debris. Now how could this be overcome? There was only one way, and that was to remove the rubbish one bucketful at a time. So likewise this is the only way we can work through our problems.

"Success," says Booker T. Washington, "is to be measured not so much by the position that one has reached in life as by the obstacles which he has overcome while trying to succeed."

"It is easy enough to be pleasant
    When life flows by like a song
But the man worthwhile
Is the man who can smile
    When everything goes dead wrong."

The Importance of The Word

The whole message of the writer of the book of Hebrews was to remind his readers that they have need of patient endurance and must not give up their reward. He writes: "But call to remembrance the former days, in which, after ye were illuminated, ye endured a great fight of afflictions; partly, whilst ye were made a gazing-stock both by reproaches and afflictions; and partly, whilst ye became companions of them that were so used. For ye had compassion of me in my bonds, and took joyfully the spoiling of your goods, knowing in yourselves that ye have in heaven a better and an enduring substance. Cast not away therefore your confidence, which hath great recompence of reward. For ye have need of patience, that, after ye have done the will of God, ye might receive the promise" (Hebrews 10:32-36).

This is also our need, and the whole Word of God is given to us to instruct and teach us that we might not fail (2 Timothy 3:16-17). "Whatsoever things were written aforetime were written for our learning, that we through patience and comfort of the scriptures might have hope" (Romans 15:4). An anonymous writer has given us some timely advice.

If you are impatient, sit down quietly and talk with Job.
If you are just a little strong-headed, go and see Moses.
If you are getting weak-kneed, take a good look at Elijah.
If there is no song in your heart, listen to David.

If you are a policy man, read Daniel.

If you are getting sordid, spend a while with Isaiah.

If your faith is below par, read Paul.

If you are getting lazy, watch James.

If you are losing sight of the future, climb up the stairs of Revelation and get a glimpse of the promised land.

The Importance of One Day at a Time

A patient that had met with a serious accident asked his doctor: "Doc, how long will I have to lie here?"

Wisely, his doctor replied: "Only one day at a time."

We cannot live any more than this, and our Savior warned us about the danger of trying to do otherwise. He said: "Sufficient unto the day is the evil thereof" (Matthew 6:34). This statement is found in the context of the Sermon on the Mount were the Lord's disciples are to trust God for everything and not to be anxious about tomorrow. The point is that there is enough evil for today about which we *are* to be concerned that we do not need to borrow any from tomorrow. But there is something else significant about this. It is only for the immediate things of the present that "grace" has been given to us. When the Lord said to Paul, "My grace is sufficient for thee" (2 Corinthians 12:9), He was calling him to bear a thorn in the flesh then, not something that *he might* call him to endure eventually. When we worry, we normally are taking something of tomorrow that *may* come upon us but which has not actually arrived. It is only potentially possible that we might have to bear it; but for such, no grace is ever given.

Borrowing evil from tomorrow is a sin and a trap from Satan, and here is why. Since the mind treats tomorrow's burden as a reality and no grace is given to bear it, we feel God has forsaken us and not provided for what we have to go through. We then doubt God's goodness and love, and by so doing, cut ourselves off from the only One who can help us; we are then taken captive by Satan. He can at this point do anything he wants with us unless we realize our sin, confess it, and get right with God. The Lord knew what He was doing when He told us: "Take therefore no thought for the morrow: for the morrow shall take thought for the things of itself. Sufficient unto the day is the evil thereof" (Matthew 6:34). Someone has put it: "Worry is like a rocking chair; it gives you something to do but doesn't get you anywhere." We can add: yet it does get you somewhere and it is to be cradled right in the lap of Satan (cf. 1 John 5:19 Gk.).

We are dealing with a subject in which there is no end, for the whole purpose of the Word of God is to encourage us to continue on as a good soldier until victory is ours, as a pilgrim until we stand on a new shore, as an ambassador until that time we can say with Paul: "I have fought a good fight, I have finished my course, I have kept the faith: henceforth there is laid up for me a crown of righteousness, which the Lord, the righteous judge, shall give me at that day: and not to me only, but unto all them also that love his appearing" (2 Timothy 4:7-8).

"A father and two children, a boy of eight and a girl of ten years, all good swimmers, entered the waters of the Atlantic at a New Jersey seashore resort a few summers ago. When some distance from shore, they became separated and the father realized they were being carried out to sea by the tide. He called out to the little girl: 'Mary, I am going to shore for help. If you get tired, turn on your back. You can float all day on your back. I'll come back for you.'

"Before long, many searchers in boats were scurrying over the face of the Atlantic Ocean hunting for one small girl, while hundreds of people to whom the news had spread waited anxiously on shore. It was four hours before they found her, far from land. She was calmly swimming on her back and was not at all frightened. Cheers and tears of joy and relief greeted the rescuers with their precious burden as they came to land.

The child took it calmly. She said, 'Daddy said he would come for me, and that I could float all day, so I swam and floated, because I knew he would come."

This is a true account given on a life insurance leaflet.

Do we really need anything more than His Word to us? He has said: "Behold I come quickly: hold that fast which thou hast, that no man take thy crown" (Revelation 3:11).

7

FORGETTING

LAW #7   WE CANNOT DO ANYTHING ABOUT LAST
YEAR'S HARVEST, BUT WE CAN ABOUT
THIS YEAR'S.

The writer of Hebrews says: "For the earth which
drinketh in the rain that cometh oft upon it, and bringeth
forth herbs meet for them by whom it is dressed, receiveth
blessing from God: but that which beareth thorns and
briars is rejected, and is nigh unto cursing; whose end is to
be burned" (Hebrews 6:7-8). Here two types of people are
analyzed. Both are the same in that they have "ground"
that will grow things and in that they receive abundantly
from God rain, sunshine and all that is needed to grow a
full harvest of the good. But that is where the similarity
ends and the distinctions begin. The one will take both
what he has as a potential and what He receives daily from
God and use them to produce fruits, grains and vegetables
that will be useful to others. On the other hand, the second
person uses the very same conditions and produces the
thorn bush, the tumble weed, the briar bush—things which
have no value whatever but are products of the curse. All
that may be done with such things is to burn them and try
in this way to put an end to their multiplying themselves
upon the land.

What an illustration this is, and what tremendous truth
it depicts! In this Scriptural analogy we have the expression
of the seventh and final law of the harvest. This seventh
law gathers together into one and completes the entire

picture presented in the truths of the other laws of the harvest.

LAW #7. WE CANNOT DO ANYTHING ABOUT LAST YEAR'S HARVEST, BUT WE CAN ABOUT THIS YEAR'S.

Whatever we did last year, last month, last week, even yesterday is over and past. Nothing we do today can in any way change the record of what was sown and what was or will be reaped as a consequence. It is either a harvest that will be worthy of praise or burning—or perhaps portions of both—but whatever was produced stands as the record of our lives lived on this earth. The problem with all too many Christians is that they are not forgetting the past and reaching on to what is before (cf. Philippians 3:13-14).

If we failed to produce a crop worthy of the Lord's praise last year our brooding and wallowing in self-pity for having wasted this time will only cause us to fail to produce anything glorifying to the Lord this year. If we did use the opportunities the Lord gave us and produced a harvest of good things, we cannot rest on our laurels. This is another year; and just because the Holy Spirit led and blessed last year, as we were obedient to Him and the Word, does not mean that we automatically will produce anything good this year.

Our Lord said: "Without me ye can do nothing" (John 15:5); and it is so true that, without abiding in Him right now, all *we* produce is wood, hay and stubble—things that will not abide the fire (cf. 1 Corinthians 3:11-15). Too many have a testimony of what the Lord did at sometime past, rather than what He is doing right now in their lives. The need for every one of us is to follow the admonition of the writer of Hebrews when he said, "Let us go on" (Hebrews 6:1). This illustration of the land producing things of blessing or cursing, and the injunction for us to go on are found in the same passage in Hebrews. We need to examine the entire context in detail in order to understand the writer's argument.

The Overview of Hebrews

The writer of the book of Hebrews has presented the truth that the Lord Jesus Christ is so much greater than any being which existed in time past. Angels had an important and significant ministry in the Old Testament, but angels are only servants of God carrying out what He desires. However, the Lord Jesus is the Son, the God of creation who never changes and who will some day rule over all (Hebrews 1:4-14; cf. Colossians 1:16-17). Yet the One who was God (cf. Hebrews 1:8) took on flesh and blood in order to minister in a way no angel could. Angels could not do anything about death, nor could they bring us to glory (Hebrews 2:5-10). Angels could not destroy him who had the power of death, that is the devil, and deliver us from his bondage; but the Son did (2:14-15). No angelic being is capable of understanding us when we sin, for none of the holy angels who are with God today ever sinned; but the Son, being a man, does understand—even though He Himself is without sin—and He comes to our aid when we are tempted (2:17-18).

Moses also, to the Hebrews, was a great man, being the one who under God led the children of Israel out of Egypt and established them as a nation. But the Son is so much greater than Moses, who was only a servant of the Lord in the House of Israel. The Lord Jesus Christ was the Builder or Creator of that House and was the exalted Son over the Nation (3:1-6). Therefore, if Moses' word needed to be heeded, how much more do the words of the Son need to be heeded today lest anyone fail because of unbelief (3:7—4:7).

Moreover, even though the Israelites followed Joshua into the land, they never enjoyed permanent peace and rest; but Jesus—the Greek equivalent for the Hebrew name, Joshua—can and does give perfect rest to everyone because He has ceased from working and has shown this by being seated upon a throne (4:8-13; cf. 1:3, 13). This makes Him, then, a greater high priest than Aaron, because under the Levitical system no seat was provided for the priest to sit upon since his work was *never* done. The place He ministers is also better than that of Aaron, being heaven itself (4:14); the person is greater, being the very Son of God who is without sin Himself (4:14-15); and His work is infinitely superior, because of the compassion He feels (4:15); and the mercy and grace He provides to the believer (4:16). Nothing like this was ever known in Israel.

The qualification for a priest was that he must be a man (5:1-2), must offer sacrifice (5:3), and must be called by God Himself (5:4). The Son has all these qualifications, yet He was called of God to be a priest of a different order than that of Aaron (5:5-10). He was "called of God an high priest after the order of Melchizedek" (5:10).

The author has much he wants to say upon the significant fact that Jesus Christ was not called to the Aaronic priesthood, but to an entirely different order; yet he will not discuss this until Chapter 7. He interrupts his teaching to make a personal application. We might even say he stops preaching and goes to meddling. Knowing all about his readers, the author realizes that it is useless for him to go on teaching without correcting a problem. It is not just more facts that they need, but the application of facts to their lives. Here is where we need to examine carefully all that is being said.

The Message of Hebrews 5:11–6:8

In Hebrews 5, verses 11 and 12 read: "Of whom [i.e. Melchizedek] we have many things to say, and hard to be uttered, seeing ye are dull of hearing. For when for the time ye ought to be teachers, ye have need that one teach you again which be the first principles of the oracles of God; and are become such as have need of milk, and not strong meat."

When teaching the book of Hebrews, I enjoy starting off in a class of Bible study having each person do some individual research. Dividing a class into five or six groups and assigning to each group a specific segment of the epistle, I ask the students to approach this book as if they had never read or heard it before. They know nothing about anything (which may be actually the case with some, but they do not want to admit it). The one question they are to search for in the book concerns the recipients: "Are they saved or lost?" "What is their spiritual condition?"

Doing this many times with various groups I have found the result is always the same. The evidence overwhelmingly is that the writer knew his recipients intimately and thoroughly, and he considered them *saved.* Certain sections of the epistle develop this truth more than others, it is readily agreed. For example, from Chapter 10 verse 19 on, one statement after another shows they had access into the very holiest place of all because they were believer-priests. The exhortations to draw near, to hold fast, to provoke unto love and good works can only be used of believers. Judgment would come to them because the Lord judges *His* people. They were to call to remembrance when they were first enlightened and so understood that Jesus Christ was the Messiah—an experience that could only happen once in a life. They had need of patience, not of salvation; of laying aside every weight, not of coming to Christ; of understanding that when God disciplines them He was dealing with them as sons; of realizing they had come "to God . . . to Jesus . . . to the blood . . . " (Hebrews 12:22-24).

On and on the references go establishing the relationship these Hebrew believers had with the Lord and His salvation. Even in the passage in Hebrews 5 that we have before us, the exhortation is *to be teachers,* not to come to salvation. No unsaved person could possibly be exhorted to be a teacher. But the problem with the recipients of this letter is that they had been saved for such a long time and attended so many courses at the Jerusalem Bible Institute that they should have been teaching others. Yet they still did not know the very elementary truths, to say nothing of the significance and implication of these truths which they had been taught. In point, they had actually sat, soaked and soured. Since a person does not develop callouses on his seat, the writer says you have become "dull of hearing" —a medical term for "old ears." They had developed a callousness of the ears and needed to go back and be taught all over again, literally, the ABC's of the Word of God. They needed to be bottle fed spiritually, because they would regurgitate solid food.

"For everyone that useth milk is unskillful in the word of righteousness: for he is a babe. But strong meat [or 'food'] belongeth to them that are of full age, even those who by reason of use have their senses exercised to discern both good and evil" (Hebrews 5:13-14). The reason they were still in babyhood spiritually was they had never used the Word they learned; and the great principle of the Christian life is *use or lose.* God had provided everything for their maturity, but they had failed to apply it to their lives. Their problem was not just a matter of knowledge; but it was a matter of their "use" or "exercise" of that knowledge in life situations, discerning what was right and wrong by the Word. A mature person is not mature because he knows a great number of facts. He is mature because he can relate the facts of Scripture to experience and so solve problems in daily living. By use of the Word, he is able to distinguish between that which is good and that which is intrinsically and basically wrong.

Since this is true—namely that the Hebrew believers needed to go on in their Christian experience—the writer continues by exhorting them toward this end in Chapter 6. "Therefore leaving the principles of the doctrine of Christ, let us go on unto perfection [maturity]" (Hebrews 6:1a). The "therefore" follows in light of what was previously stated about their babyhood. They were not only to go on from the ABC's concerning the teaching of the Messiah, but go on to maturity, becoming full grown, useful Christians who could know and apply the whole of truth. "Not laying again the foundation of repentance from dead works, and of faith toward God, of the doctrine of baptisms, and of laying on of hands, and of resurrection of the dead, and of eternal judgment. And this we will do, if God permit" (Hebrews 6:1b-3).

There is absolutely nothing wrong with knowing these six basic and foundational truths, for these were the very things that figured prominently in the teachings and activities of the early chruch as seen in the book of Acts. The foundation is fine; but if you continue to lay foundation upon foundation, you build a monstrosity. You need to lay the foundation and then *go on;* and this "going on" we will do if God wills it. We may have wasted so much time that our life may be over before we come to know and use the Word in a mature way; yet whatever time we have, *let us go on.*

What follows continues the same thought which is emphasized by the word "for." This gives us in a statement why we are to "go on." "For it is impossible . . ." Something here is completely and totally impossible and this is why we must go on. This word "impossible" stands here at the very head of the sentence and governs all that will be said. Here is something completely impossible. In all the years of time and eternity, this could never be done. It is a construction like Hebrews 10:4, "For it is not possible that the blood of bulls and of goats should take away sins." How many animal sacrifices would it take to have sins completely taken away? Could it be done in time itself? Not on your life, for in all of time or eternity animal sacrifices could never take away sin. But what was impossible for the blood of bulls and goats to do, the man Jesus Christ did in "one sacrifice for sins for ever" (Hebrews 10:12).

But what is impossible here in Hebrews 6? It is impossible for certain ones who have five specific things stated about them to do something. Who are these that are referred to as those who (1) "were once enlightened"; (2) "have tasted of the heavenly gift"; (3) "were made partakers of the Holy Spirit"; (4) "have tasted the good word of God"; and (5) "the powers of the world to come [the coming age]?" The book of Hebrews itself defines these terms and in this way identifies who these persons are. First, in Hebrews 10:32 the author says, "But call to remembrance the former days, in which, after ye were illuminated [same word 'enlightened'], ye endured a great fight of afflictions." This word "enlighten" describes the moment the light of the gospel was apprehended by us for the first time (cf. 2 Corinthians 4:4, 6; Ephesians 3:9; 2 Timothy 1:10). It is a "once" enlightenment that can never be repeated, in just the same way that the sacrifice of Christ is "once for all" (cf. Hebrews 9:7, 26; 10:2; 12:26). The light of the gospel can never come to a person more than once.

Secondly, these "have tasted of the heavenly gift." In Hebrews 2:9, when Jesus tasted death for every man, He did not put it to His lips and then cast it aside. He completely devoured it. "Tasting," in the Greek language, signifies holding something in common with someone else. Christ partook of death for us completely so that we might partake of the gift of eternal life completely. God's gifts and calling are without repentance on God's part (Romans 11:29), for He does not begin a work and not bring it to completion. He never wishes He had not done something. What we hold in common with heaven is that we have been given eternal life as our possession, and it is ours. We hold this life in common with Jesus Christ so that His very life for all eternity is now our life on earth in time. He died our death and we now have His life (cf. Galatians 2:20).

Thirdly, "and were made partakers of the Holy Spirit." The word "partakers" is used in Hebrews 2:14; 3:1 and 14 and signifies in all these verses more than just participation. It is rather the personal character that has been gained because of vital relationship. For instance, the personal characteristic of the human race was that of flesh and blood; and it was this in which Christ took a vital, real, personal part and so "partook." Thus, to be partakers of the Holy Spirit is to have the Holy Spirit govern one's life. Such an experience commences with what Scripture calls "regeneration" when we are born again by the Holy Spirit of God (cf. John 3:6, 8; Romans 8:9).

The word "taste" governs both the fourth and fifth statement. These "have tasted of the good word of God." Only the child of God has a capacity to devour the Word of God and know verily that it is manna from heaven for us who are pilgrims.

Lastly, regarding "the powers of the coming age," i.e. the powers of the millennial age, they had not partaken of the coming age, but of the powers of that age in experiencing the new birth in their own lives and His working in behalf of believers.

The five things stated here could only be stated of believers, and that is exactly what the writer wants to convey. There is something specifically impossible for believers to do who have been saved; and since something is impossible for a saved person to do, there is only one other alternative and that is to *go on.* Everyone of these five statements is in the aorist tense in the original language, signifying that these things are never repeated acts of God's working. If the Hebrews had not been *babes* and born again, they could have experienced these things; but since they had been saved, these five acts had occurred in their lives and could not occur again.

Then, what is he saying is impossible? It is impossible for those who are saved "if they shall fall away, to renew them again unto repentance; seeing they crucify to themselves the Son of God afresh, and put him to an open shame" (Hebrews 6:6). The "if" is not in the original, but is supplied; and the "impossible" still governs all that is being said. Literally it reads: "And having fallen away to renew again to repentance. . ." The word "repentance" has been used in context (Hebrews 6:1) of a repentance from dead works to a salvation experience, and this is the way the word is used many times in the New Testament. It would, therefore, appear from the context that this is the way the author is using the word "repentance" here.

It is impossible for a saved person to fall out of salvation and then be saved again, because in order for him to be saved a second time, he would have to have the Lord Jesus Christ die all over again. This would be testifying that His first death was insufficient to do a perfect work in reference to sin. If he had to die a second time, what about a third time and a fourth? Thus, there is only one direction a believer—a babe living in immaturity—can go, and that is *on.*

When we come to Christ as a sinner, He forgives us all our sins and gives us a fresh new life and start. This is wonderful. But since that time we have not gone on but have lapsed into immaturity, not using the Word in discerning the difference between the things that are good and the things that actually "ought not to be." Yet we *cannot* come to another cross experience and be saved all over again, having the years of our babyhood erased. The record of our immaturity stands; and since we cannot have it removed, there is only one way we can go—"Let us go on to maturity."

We might diagram it this way.

This is impossible:

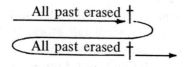

Therefore this must be done:

So we have come back to the illustration found in Hebrews 6:7 and 8 with which we began. The analogy fits perfectly where two individuals have the potential of producing "fruit" to the praise and glory of God. One does this, but the other takes the same provisions and produces that which must be burned. It is the fruit of the ground that is rejected and burned; *land* itself does not burn. It is not the believer that is going to burn, but the believer's works even as Paul says in 1 Corinthians 3. "Every man's work shall be made manifest: for the day shall declare it, because it shall be revealed by fire; and the fire shall try every man's work of what sort it is. If any man's work abide . . . he shall receive a reward. If any man's work shall be burned, he shall suffer loss: but he himself shall be saved; yet so as by fire" (3:13-15).

The Truth Applied

Now if we are not able to make application of the Word in a practical way to our own lives, we are no better than the immature Hebrews. There is not a believer alive that does not have some wasted time, and perhaps many have wasted years. I have; but there is nothing I can do about those wasted years. What I can do by the grace of God is so live now that I produce a full harvest that will glorify the Savior. This is what we all are to do. Regardless of where we are in the Christian life, regardless of how much time we have wasted, regardless of the terrible products we have produced in our lives—we are to go on to maturity. This is the Spirit's exhortation to all of us.

We come then to the same truth emphasized in the sixth law, namely we must forget about the past and concentrate on that which is at hand. The "Illinois Medical Journal" carried an article that states why this is so important.

"There are two days in every week about which we should not worry—two days which should be kept from fear and apprehension.

"One of these days is Yesterday with its mistakes and cares, its aches and pains, its faults and blunders. Yesterday has passed forever beyond our control.

"All the money in the world cannot bring back Yesterday. We cannot undo a single act we performed; we cannot erase a single word we said. Yesterday is gone.

"The other day we should not worry about is Tomorrow with its possible adversities, its burdens, its large promise and poor performance. Tomorrow is beyond our immediate control.

"Tomorrow's sun will rise either in splendor or behind a mask of clouds—but it will rise. Until it does, we have no stake in Tomorrow, for it is as yet unborn.

"That leaves only one day—Today. Any man, by the grace of God, can fight the battles of just one day. It is only when you and I add the burdens of those two awful eternities—Yesterday and Tomorrow—that we break down.

"It is not the experience of Today that drives men mad—it is remorse or bitterness for something which happened Yesterday and the dread of what Tomorrow may bring. Let us, therefore, journey but one day at a time."

There is one point in which all of us are the same that may be illustrated in the following way. Let's say a bank credited to your account every day $86,400 without fail. Yet the bank carried over no balance from day to day, and so allowed you to keep no cash in your account. What was not used of the $86,400 was lost by days end, yet for the next day you had a new credit in your account. This is exactly what happens to each of us as God credits to our account each day 86,400 seconds of time. We either use time properly or we lose it, for the day cannot be relived again. Each day is a new day with new opportunities, but once we move through the day our record stands. This is the reason Paul gave an admonishment to believers in Ephesians 5, "Awake thou that sleepest, and arise from the dead, and Christ shall give thee light. See then that ye walk circumspectly, not as fools, but as wise, redeeming the time, because the days are evil" (vv. 14-16).

No person alive can say he has "no time," for time is the one thing we all have equally. Nor can anyone "kill time" because it keeps right on going on. We may waste time or choose to do one thing rather than another, but we need to learn to use time to its fullest so that at the end of our days we may say, "I have finished my course" (2 Timothy 4:7). To do this, we must be able both to distinguish the things that differ and "approve the things that are excellent" (Philippians 1:10). This involves two things: (1) Knowing and using the Word and (2) disciplining ourselves in our problem areas. The matter of discipline is what makes the difference because a disciplined person will use the Word. This is what makes him disciplined.

The Need for Self-discipline

The "War Cry" magazine reminds us of an important principle. "A loose wire gives out no musical note; but fasten the ends, and the piano, the harp, or the violin is born. Free steam drives no machine, but hamper and confine it with piston and turbine and you have the great world of machinery made possible. The unhampered river drives no dynamos, but dam it up and we get power sufficient to light a great city. So our lives must be disciplined if we are to be of any real service in this world."

Paul said to the Corinthians: "Know ye not that they which run in a race run all, but one receiveth the prize? So run, that ye may obtain. And every man that striveth for the mastery is temperate ['controls himself'] in all things. Now they do it to obtain a corruptible crown; but we an incorruptible. I therefore so run, not as uncertainly; so fight I, not as one that beateth the air: but I keep under [buffet] my body, and bring it into subjection: lest that by any means, when I have preached to others, I myself should be a castaway ['disapproved,' 'disqualified'] (1 Corinthians 9:24-27).

Every two years there was celebrated near Corinth the Isthmian games which involved five sports: Leaping, discus throwing, racing, boxing and wrestling. The athlete who was proclaimed the victor appeared before the judges sitting on the Bema seat, and he was awarded a wreath of pine leaves (winners in the Olympian games were awarded a wreath from the wild olive tree). Athletes who trained for ten months prior to the contest would discipline themselves to such an extent that anything that might hinder their winning, however good it might be otherwise, was set aside. They did this for a temporal passing honor.

Paul, however, was involved in a far greater and higher contest, and he was out to win. He would "buffet" his body to keep it in subjection to himself, rather than have his body control and dictate to him. The word "buffet" signifies to "strike under the eye, give a black eye to." This is exactly what it takes to control the body along with the tongue which is the last member to be brought under control of the Spirit of God (cf. James 3:1-10). Paul did all this so that he would not be one who would herald out to others "the rules" of the race, and then not follow himself the very rules he announced to others. If he failed to follow the rules, he would be disapproved or disqualified at the end of the contest and so would not receive the award. All too many have failed in this very thing because they have failed to discipline themselves.

If you can learn to keep your head while others are losing theirs, you will be a head taller than everyone else. A woman who apologized flippantly for her frequent flare-ups said: "Well, one good thing, they're always over in a minute." Her pastor would not let her get by that easily and replied: "So is a shotgun blast, but it blows everything to pieces." There may be many things we cannot control that come upon us, but we should never let another person determine how we are going to act. All too often we only *react* rather than consciously and purposefully acting in accordance with our high calling in Christ Jesus.

We cannot control the length of our life,
    but we can control its width and depth.
We cannot control the contour of our countenance,
    but we can control its expression.
We cannot control the other person's annoying habits,
    but we can do something about our own.
We cannot control the distance our head is above
    the ground,
      but we can control the height of the contents we
      feed into it.
God help us do something about what we can control
    and leave all else in the hands of God!

There is the discipline of our lives that we are to do, and there is the discipline that God Himself does. An unknown author wrote:

"The tests of life are to make, not break us. Trouble may demolish a man's business but build up his character. The blow at the outward man may be the greatest blessing to the inner man. If God, then, puts or permits anything hard in our lives, be sure that the real peril, the real trouble is what we shall lose if we flinch or rebel."

Whom God uses, He takes and disciplines (cf. Hebrews 12:5-11). We see this in all the men and women of both the Old and New Testaments. Before Abraham could be blessed by God, he had to get rid of the old life and the lie connected with it (Genesis 20:1-18). Before Jacob was a "prince with God," the rebel had to be taken out of this man so that he walked humbly before his God (Genesis 32:1-32). Before Joseph was exalted, he had to deal not only with the issues of what his brothers had done to him in selling him for twenty pieces of silver, but what God Himself had allowed to come into his life. He was faithful under discipline and trial and then was exalted by God. The same is true of Moses, of David, of Daniel, and of everyone else whom God uses. Each person is a unique story in itself right along with the New Testament personages of Peter, John, Paul and the others.

> For every hill I've had to climb,
>> For every stone that bruised my feet,
> For all the blood and sweat and grime,
>> For blinding storms and heat,
> My heart sings but a grateful song—
>> These were the things that made me strong!
> For all the heartaches and the tears,
>> For all the anguish and the pain,
> For gloomy days and fruitless years,
>> And for the hopes that lived in vain,
> I do give thanks, for now I know
>> These were the things that helped me grow!
> 'Tis not the softer things of life
>> Which stimulate man's will to strive;
> But bleak adversity and strife
>> Do most to keep man's will alive.
> O'er rose-strewn paths the weaklings creep,
>> But brave hearts dare to climb the steep.
>> —Author Unknown

God is concerned in building into us character. To do this, He sends into our lives unique and trying experiences, tempered for each of us as individuals so that we not only are not overwhelmed and discouraged by the severity of the trials (cf. 1 Corinthians 10:13), but we are not so free that we forget our constant need and dependency upon Him.

"Character is like a tree," said Abraham Lincoln, "and reputation like its shadow. The shadow is what we think of it: the tree is the real thing."

"Too many people," says "The Bulletin," "are more concerned about their reputation—what people think—than they are their character. Many a godly person has been falsely accused and his reputation blackened. They called Christ a glutton and a wine-bibber and a friend of publicans and sinners! Major on character—what God sees—and everything else will be right. To pretend to be what we are not is to rot away at the heart. But to strive to be what God wants us to be is to build a life for His glory. People can ruin your reputation. Only *you* can ruin your character."

Henry G. Bosch, writing in *Our Daily Bread,* says: "A successful Christian is one who by the grace of God can lay a firm foundation for a better life with the 'bricks' that others throw at him!"

Keys for Growth and Maturity

Discipline produces character which produces fruitfulness. Discipline is the major key in forgetting the past and reaching forth unto the good works that are before us in the will and plan of God. Discipline involves every aspect of our lives. It begins with accepting what God brings into our lives as coming from a God of infinite love, goodness, justice, and holiness together with all the other attributes of His being. This is first and primary, for whenever the enemy can get us to doubt the goodness and love of our God, everything about us caves in. Discipline involves all things involved in time, particularly all that we feed into our minds. This is why we are continually to be renewing our mind upon the Lord (Romans 12:2), thinking upon things that are true, honest, just, pure, lovely, of good report, virtuous and praiseworthy (Philippians 4:8). He has promised to keep in perfect peace those whose mind is stayed on Him (Isaiah 26:3). The Word needs to be our meditation day and night (Psalm 1:2), for when this is done we shall have a prosperous and fruitful life (Psalm 1:3).

Discipline ends with our controlling ourselves, and here again Satan "overwhelms us" with the magnitude of the problem. Since there is so much to do, the tendency is that we do nothing. Or we come to a place where we surrender everything to God, only to find that the flesh then not only begins to exert itself all the stronger, but it rises up and defeats us. Or we set out to accomplish a complete and dramatic change in ourselves which lasts from 60 minutes to

60 hours, and then we blow the whole thing. In blowing it we become so discouraged we feel worse than before.

If these are your experiences, you are a normal Christian; but you still need to press on. Rather than try to bring under discipline all aspects of your life, work on one thing. Do not bite off a bigger hunk than you can chew. If you feel the need for having a time of devotions in the morning, do not set the alarm for 4:30. You will keep the appointment for only two days before you sleep in and chuck the whole procedure. Set the alarm only five minutes, or at the most ten minutes, earlier than usual; *and then get up.* Make it a habit by doing this for a month. Now you are ready to increase the time five more minutes if you desire. The point is to keep on working and moving constantly by appropriating the Word into your life. The man who stops working starts deteriorating.

Let Us Go On

Seek to acquire a balance in your life by reading all the Word and meditating therein. Strive for the high calling of being conformed to the image of God's dear Son. Dr. Vernon Mortenson has stated the *high requirements for high service* for which all of us should strive. We should be:

Self-reliant but not self-sufficient
Energetic but not self-seeking
Steadfast but not stubborn
Tactful but not timid
Serious but not sullen
Loyal but not sectarian
Unmovable but not stationary
Gentle but not hypersensitive
Tenderhearted but not touchy
Conscientious but not a perfectionist
Disciplined but not demanding
Generous but not gullible
Meek but not weak
Humorous but not hilarious

Friendly but not familiar
Holy but not holier-than-thou
Discerning but not critical
Progressive but not pretentious

May we keep the ideal ever before us, remembering that as we behold the Lord in the Word and in prayer we will be changed more and more into His likeness (2 Corinthians 3:18). Whatever you do, give yourself time to grow. Reject every gimmick for instant maturity. It takes time to become a man of God, and there are no short cuts. Remember that God can make a squash in about three months time, but it takes Him a hundred years to make an oak. If you want to be blessed of God, you must work in accordance with His laws of the harvest; for He will not change them for anyone. God grant that your life will count in a positive way for the Savior.

If you can keep the faith when those about you
Are losing it and seeking something new:
If you can stand the firmer though they flout you
As being simple and old-fashioned too;

If you can put your hand in Christ's and, feeling
The marks of Calvary's scars upon your palm,
Can gladly say "Amen" to all His dealing,
Or change the sigh into a joyous psalm;

If you can laugh when human hopes are banished,
When castles fall and cherished prospects die:
And just keep on, though earthly props have vanished,
Content to see the pattern by and by;

If you can meet abuse without complaining
And greet your unkind critic with a smile,
If, conscious that your human love is waning,
You claim a Calvary love that knows no guile;

If you can bear the unjust imputation,
Without a murmur or revengeful thought,
And even forfeit rights and reputation,
Because His glory is the one thing sought;

If you can give an honest commendation
To him whose work looms larger than your own,
Or scorn to speak the word of condemnation
To him who falls or reaps what he has sown;

If you can give consent to Calvary's dying
And live again in resurrection power,
If you can claim the victory, not by trying,
But resting in His triumph every hour;

If you can be content with His provision,
Though others seem to prosper and succeed;
Nor let repining mar the heavenly vision,
And simply trust in God for every need;

If you can let the mind of Christ possess you,
To think on "things of good report" and true;
And ever let the love of Christ obsess you,
Constraining everything you say and do;

If you can find in Him your highest treasure,
Commit to Him your thoughts, your fears, your
    frown,
Then life is yours, and blessing without measure,
And—what is more—you'll wear the victor's crown.
                          —Author Unknown

SCRIPTURE INDEX

Scripture Index

Scripture Index